P9-CAA-006

PROPHETIC EVANGELISM

EMPOWERING A GENERATION TO SEIZE THEIR DAY

PROPHETIC EVANGELISM

EMPOWERING A GENERATION TO SEIZE THEIR DAY

SEAN SMITH

Destiny Image® **Publishers, Inc.**
P.O. Box 310
Shippensburg, PA 17257-0310

"Speaking to the Purposes of God for This Generation
and for the Generations to Come"

ISBN 0-7684-2335-X

For Worldwide Distribution
Printed in the U.S.A.

4 5 6 7 8 / 09

This book and all other Destiny Image, Revival Press, MercyPlace, Fresh Bread, Destiny Image Fiction, and Treasure House books are available at Christian bookstores and distributors worldwide.

For a U.S. bookstore nearest you, call
1-800-722-6774.
For more information on foreign distributors, call
717-532-3040.
Or reach us on the Internet:
www.destinyimage.com

DEDICATION

I dedicate this book to my grandmother, Ethel Wynn, who carried the presence of Jesus when I needed to see a tangible expression. I dedicate this book to all evangelists, campus pastors, soul winners, and outreach directors, who give their all every day without much fanfare or recognition. I also especially dedicate this project to my children—both biological and spiritual—take it to the next level! Finally, I dedicate this work to all who have supported us over the years.

ACKNOWLEDGMENTS

There are many special people who invested in the development of this project. There are also many whom I would like to thank because without them I would not have been in a position to tackle this challenging work.

Barb—My wife, soul mate, and my babe; you have been the most awesome godly wife a man could ever have. Thank you for believing in me.

Brandon and Brittany—I am so grateful that God has blessed my life with such a wonderful son and daughter. Thanks for going after God with all of your hearts. The sky is truly the limit for you guys. Daddy loves you.

Nina Walls—Thanks, Mom, for your model of sacrifice and love, which helped get me through so much.

Mike and Michelle Kennedy—I'm so taken aback by the countless hours you have spent transcribing, organizing, and managing our first book. You guys are incredible! Thanks for your encouragement and sensitivity.

Frank and Kendra Raya—You are the best in-laws a brother could have. Thanks so much for believing in our lives and for your consistent investment in this ministry.

Liberty Savard—Thanks so much for all of your last-minute help; you were truly God's closer in this project.

My thanks also to these special people:
— Gaylord and Patti Enns, Francisco and Toni Escobedo, Jeff and M.J. Rostocil, and Darwin and Yolanda Benjamin.

— Sam and Linda Huddleston, Mario Murillo, Donnie and Cindy Moore, and Pastor Paul and Denise Goulet.
— Pastor Che and Sue Ahn, Pastor Tommy Barnett, Mike Bickle, and Napoleon Kaufman.
— Scott Martin, Chi Alpha Ministries, Pastor Ron Eviaz, and Pastor Ken Hubbard.
— Pastor Bill Bates, Pastor Eugene and Joyce Kraft, and Jim and Jane Manley.
— Steven and Katherena Higashi, Doug and Crystal Heisel, Pastor Ron Pinkston, and Stephen and Carol Angove.

Dee Davis—Thanks for your intercession. Also, thanks to all of our intercessors and Pointblank Partners who love and support us with their prayers and finances.

Jesus—Most of all, I am indebted and eternally grateful to You, my Majestic King and Deliverer. I praise You, for You alone are worthy. Thanks for putting the call of God on my broken life. You rescued me so I could help rescue others!

ENDORSEMENTS

Sean Smith is a man on fire for God, a man with a passion for lost souls. Sean has a prophetic vision for evangelism. Few today have this prophetic/evangelistic ministry.

Read *Prophetic Evangelism* and see what the Spirit is saying to the Church for these last days. The heartbeat of God is the Great Commission, which is made clear in Revelation. That is why we must hear the voice of God, and know what the Bible says about the day we live in and what is coming to pass on planet earth. All hell is about to break loose, but God has an awesome plan for those who love Him.

Jim Bakker
Author and Speaker

I have known Sean for many years and see an unusual zeal and anointing on his life for evangelism. He carries a fire for reaching this generation. This book, *Prophetic Evangelism*, combines bridal affections for Jesus with prophetic power to present Jesus as the Lamb to unbelievers. This is not a book of evangelism theories, but incarnate truths that will equip you to seize this generation for eternity. Sean lives out what he says. This book addresses the reality of giving a supernatural witness of Christ, as well as gives practical insight. I highly recommend this book!

Mike Bickle
Director of the International House of Prayer
Kansas City, MO

Sean Smith has given the 21st-century Church a radical and much-needed new perspective on the all-important subject of evangelism. This powerful handbook is a cutting-edge evangelistic tool for all churches that are eager to fulfill Christ's Great Commission. I highly recommend both the book and the author.

Dennis Cramer
Author and President of Dennis Cramer Ministries

Sean Smith brings a remarkable perspective and fresh insights that will compel you to reconsider the way you view evangelism. As you journey through the pages of *Prophetic Evangelism*, you will be instructed, equipped, and energized to fulfill the mandate of the Great Commission. This book stands at the top of my list of "must reads."

Marc Estes
Director of Pastoral and Harvest Ministries, City Bible Church
Portland, OR

Author of *Jesus Today*, Sean Smith is a gifted communicator who has a passion for God and a passion for the lost. He is a leading thinker and practitioner when it comes to power evangelism in the 21st century. Sean's book will inspire and challenge you to be a more effective witness to this generation. I highly recommend it.

Ken Foreman, Jr.
Senior Pastor, Cathedral of Faith
San Jose, CA

I wholeheartedly recommend Sean Smith's new book, *Prophetic Evangelism*. Sean writes from his vast experience of ministry and relationships nationwide, especially with young adults in the throes of major cultural change. He has a unique combination of a powerful prophetic ministry and an incredibly down-to-earth style that engages his audiences. He is real.

Prophetic Evangelism represents the insights and actions from the Word that Sean has experienced and learned. Sean is one of the best communicators I know and a spiritually discerning leader. I have known Sean for many years as a campus minister and evangelist, and in recent years as one of our most sought after speakers at our university student conferences held nationally. Whether speaking or writing, Sean has a message every Christian needs to hear.

Dennis Gaylor
National Director, Chi Alpha Campus Ministries USA

Read this book! Sean Smith uniquely addresses a critically urgent need in the Church today…winning the lost to Jesus Christ. Make no mistake, his intention is for you to rise up and make a difference now through spreading the gospel.

Scott Hinkle
President of Scott Hinkle Outreach Ministries
and Soulwinners International
Columnist for *Charisma Magazine*

Sean Smith is one of a small handful of people I know who are qualified to write such a book. *Prophetic Evangelism* is more than something he does; it is who he is. From the insights of Scripture to Sean's stories of personal experience, the reader is compelled to join this last-days army to change the course of history with the same tools used by Jesus.

Bill Johnson
Senior Pastor, Bethel Church
Redding, CA
Author of *When Heaven Invades Earth*

Sean has not only written an excellent book on prophetic evangelism, he exemplifies it in his everyday life. It will help you to confound the enemy.

Napoleon Kaufman
Senior Pastor, The Well Christian Community
Dublin, CA
Former NFL player

Prophetic Evangelism is about the smart bomb of soul winning. This mighty and long overdue book is not at all what you might think. Anyone who wishes to win souls and hopes for America to survive this present darkness has found their appointed reading.

So what is prophetic evangelism? Perhaps the apostle Peter best illustrates it, before and after the Day of Pentecost. His final witness before the death of Jesus consisted of standing by a fire and denying he knew Jesus with foul language. That is a weak witness! Today, many leaders salve their conscience by observing thriving mega-churches or the crowds gathering at events that carry Christian overtones. All that has really happened is that many small churches have folded into one big full-service church. The actual Christian population has gone down! We do not see a core change in the values of Americans. True conversions are rare. Like the pre-upper room Peter, we have, at best, a weak and unconvincing witness.

When Peter got on fire, he became the total opposite of the sniveling disciple he was by the fire. Now he roared with explosive precision and the people's protection from God departed. The result was quantity and quality salvations.

There remains an open door for a massive harvest and *Prophetic Evangelism* launches you through that door.

Mario Murillo
President of Mario Murillo Ministries
Author of *Fresh Fire* and *Critical Mass*

Sean Smith is a young man who, having touched Heaven, is now bent on sending a sacred fire to earth. His prophetic calling and unique giftings have taken him to the multitudes of the unchurched, unreached, and untouched youth of this emerging 21st century in the schools, streets, and cities. The operation of his life is now squarely targeted on showing God's love and power to a new generation who has never seen Christ as He really is. I recommend, without reservation, what God has done and will do through this young gladiator of the gyms, the gangs, and the ghettos of both the culture and the Church. He is a new captain in this war for the souls of those who will help carve out the history of this coming century.

Winkey Pratney
International Speaker and Author

Sean Smith exemplifies a prophetic ministry of integrity and purpose. His ability to stir others in a passionate pursuit of God's heart makes him a special gift to the Body of Christ. I personally recommend this manuscript and hope that everyone desiring a greater understanding of prophetic evangelism will read this wonderful book. It is a valuable contribution from a man whom I consider to be on the cutting edge of revival today.

Larry Randolph
President of Larry Randolph Ministries
Author of *User-Friendly Prophecy*

Sean Smith is removing the grave clothes from antiquated methods of evangelism and exposing the glory for God's heart, as it pertains to evangelism in the 21st-century Church. I believe that this dimension of evangelism will lead to another Jesus People Movement. There will be no harvest without prophetic evangelism. This is a "now" word!

Sammy Rodriguez
Founder of Third Day Believer's Network
President of the National Hispanic Christian Leadership Conference
Author of *The Third-Day Church*

Sean Smith ministered at my Mentoring Conference in Sacramento in the late 1990s. I've never felt called to be an evangelist, but after hearing Sean speak twice that day I wanted to go out and evangelize the world! This dynamic evangelist of God's end-time kingdom message has the ability to communicate passion more effectively than any other speaker I've ever heard. Sean's written words manage to ring with the same radiation of passion and reality that his preached words do. As an author and editor who is aware of what is happening in the Christian publishing business today, I can tell you that this is a rare quality. It is a remarkable platform he ministers from, speaking the truth of God in such a way that pure radiation emanates out of him with genuine reality! I'm delighted that God has also enabled Sean to capture truth and then give it out to others in a way that demands that the words within this book must be read.

Rev. Liberty Savard
President of Liberty Savard Ministries
Sacramento, CA
Author of *Shattering Your Strongholds*

Sean Smith is part of a new breed of dynamic young prophets and evangelists that God is raising up in this generation. His writings are fresh and alive with both revelation and experience. You will be equally edified and challenged. I have known this man of God for several years and have seen him to be a man of integrity and passion. I trust, as you read, that you will catch both!

Wendell Smith
Senior Pastor, The City Church
Kirkland, WA
Author of *Great Faith*

Of the key ingredients in Master's Commission, evangelism tops the list. Of the top voices speaking to Master's Commission, Sean Smith tops the list. The teachings of Sean Smith on evangelism will be read by many disciples. I believe *Prophetic Evangelism* is the final evolution of evangelism for the endtimes.

Lloyd Zeigler
Master's Commission International Director

CONTENTS

Foreword

Pastor Tommy Barnett

One of my burdens for the Body of Christ today has to do with personal evangelism—what I affectionately refer to as "soul winning." The tragic aspect is that most believers never experience the privilege and the joy of leading someone to the Lord. Some have said that less than 6 percent of those who call themselves Christians have ever led someone to the Lord. Interestingly enough, of those who do, the large majority do so in the early days of their Christian walk when their initial enthusiasm about the discovery of Christ ignites a fire in others.

I do not believe this is due to unwillingness—everyone wants to see people get saved—but due to a lack of equipping.

That's why I am so excited about this book. My friend, Sean Smith, has taken the mystery out of witnessing to people, and he makes the spiritual practical. This is an easy-to-understand yet profound exploration of a Holy Spirit-led, relevant means of seeing more souls won to Christ. Sean's infectious passion pours through this thorough explanation of how God wants to move through His people, to call people out of darkness and into His marvelous light.

Today, people are hungry for an authentic Christianity, evidenced by the power of God, and walked out in daily living. Whether it's the boardroom, the back room, or the back alley, a fitting word from Heaven, at the appropriate time, delivered in love, sets people free from their mistaken notions of Christianity. It introduces them to a consuming and fulfilling relationship.

If anyone wants to be more effective in utilizing what God calls the "power to be a witness," they must read this book. If anyone puts into practice the principles so wonderfully described herein, and will risk the obedience necessary, they will seize incredible opportunities. Additionally, God will make you aware of how to see the Holy Spirit supernaturally change lives forever. Get ready to embark on a journey that will lead you to joy and fruitfulness for the rest of your life!

Tommy Barnett
Senior Pastor, Phoenix First Assembly of God
Phoenix, AZ

FOREWORD

PASTOR CHE AHN

It was March 1973 and my best friend had bought me a ticket to the Deep Purple concert. Deep Purple was a very heavy metal, rock and roll group from England, who was going to hold a concert at the Baltimore Civic Center. We had the best seats in the house, third row from the center of the stage. During the intermission, my friends walked around while I stayed back to save the seats. During this break, I was having a debate in my mind with God.

Two weeks earlier I had cried out to God to reveal Himself to me and He did through a revelation of His love for me. For three days I could not stop weeping. I also couldn't stop doing drugs. I was a drug addict and a drug pusher. Even though God had revealed His love to me, I really didn't want to give up my partying lifestyle. I figured since God is a God of love, I could still do drugs as long as I didn't sell them.

As soon as I came to this smug conclusion, two guys I had never met before came and sat down next to me. I thought that they were trying to move to a better seat during the intermission. I was going to say that the seats were taken, but before I could get a word out, the person closest to me said, "I know what you're thinking. You think that you can party and still be right with God. But you are still far from Him."

With those words he and his friend got up and left. Needless to say I was freaked out! The conviction of God hit me so hard; I cried out to God right then and there and asked Him to show me what to do. I heard a still small voice say, "Throw away your drugs, leave this concert, and follow Me." And that is exactly what I did, and I have been following Jesus ever since.

19

The purpose of this testimony is to say that I was converted through prophetic evangelism. Some Christians who were at the concert to evangelize had "read my mail" by the Spirit of God. And as a result, I made a decision to totally follow Jesus.

Jesus said, in John 4:35, "The harvest is ripe." People now are more open to know about Jesus than ever before. Although I believe in all different types of evangelism, prophetic evangelism is so powerful because it cuts through the deception of sin and reveals a supernatural, personal God.

Sean Smith writes an outstanding book on prophetic evangelism that is not only inspirational, with all of the wonderful testimonies, but it is also a book that will equip and activate you to move in prophetic evangelism. I have many books on evangelism but I know of no other book like this one.

I have personally known Sean Smith for many years now; he is the real deal. He practices what he preaches. He is an Ephesians 4:11 evangelist who eats, breathes, and sleeps evangelism as a lifestyle. Your life will never be the same as you read this book. Let the adventure begin.

Che Ahn
Senior Pastor, Harvest Rock Church
Pasadena, CA
Founder and President of Harvest International Ministries

EZEKIEL SPEAKS

To live at a time when God turns a new page in the heavenlies, in a nation, or in a person, is a powerful blessing and realization. Today, everywhere you turn people are sensing spiritual, sociological, and ideological transitions. We are in a hallway of human history preparing to enter the threshold of a new epoch.

I believe that you are ready to break out into a larger and more significant future. We are each called to something that legitimizes the time and space we've occupied while riding this fallen planet. Often God inspires in us a "holy restlessness" while stirring deep yearnings to be a part of the mighty work He is about to do. You and I have been positioned to witness something incredible, or more accurately, to become a witness of a "God thing."

In Ezekiel 37, the prophet Ezekiel is placed in an eerily similar situation. He is positioned to view a valley of dry bones. Then God caused Ezekiel to pass by them in an intimate dynamic. His up-close, "I-see-dead-people" experience was ordained by God. This was about engagement. Ezekiel had to dive into this world and "swim" beneath the surface. God's design is to involve redeemed humanity in speaking life into deadness.

I've spent the better part of two decades observing and reaching out to college campuses, inner cities, and the well-to-do. My conclusions are varied, yet substantial. At times it can seem hopeless and unrealistic to reach any of these groups.

In Ezekiel's case, God asks him a question. This question was meant to cause Ezekiel to probe deeper into this dilemma. (Good questions work on us; we don't work on them. They become a doorway into a greater realization of something.)

Why would the Lord insist that Ezekiel get up close to see the disconnected bones? The "bare bone" facts were that they were many, and they were very dry.

I believe God's intention was to impress upon Ezekiel the full extent of the problem so that he could appreciate the full extent of the answer.

Ezekiel stared at the impossible and the improbable. This discovery did two things: (1) It caused Ezekiel to know that it wasn't about his sophisticated approach, compelling persuasiveness, or human methodology, and (2) it caused Ezekiel to become a divine agent for "dead" humanity. Ezekiel's response to God's question was "only You can answer that one."

Only God can answer the heartfelt sinister stalemate of the radically unchurched, the neo-atheist, or your lost relative. Ezekiel was told to prophesy toward that which seemingly could not hear, yet God caused them to become what was spoken. That valley went from a "to the bone" death camp to a vast vibrant army.

Prophetic evangelism is an important truth. It says: "Our deeper purpose will only find expression when we transform the culture and the institutions that we've inherited by the unique direction of the Holy Spirit." *Prophetic Evangelism* takes you on a journey of insight and discovery that communicates that there is a quality of experience waiting for you that will trigger a quantity of results. God wants you to be touched with a prophetic flow that will transform you and touch the unsaved.

The vast majority of Christians I know desire greater effectiveness and fruitfulness, yet they are in the dark as to how to accomplish it. Former efforts to share Jesus with others have produced little fruit and have even seemed counterproductive. Many of the formulas and methods we've used seem cold, rigid, and mechanical.

In the Spirit, I sense a barometric rise pointing to the release of a "new wind" of spiritual influence that will encourage a generation of harvesters to go public with their testimony of the Lord Jesus Christ. This new model of spiritual influence is based on John 5:19-20, which portrays a certain dynamic: "Then Jesus answered and said to them, 'Most assuredly, I say to you, the Son can do nothing of Himself, but what He sees the Father do; for whatever He does, the Son also does in like manner.'" It is joining in on what the Father is already doing and picking up what the Spirit is emphasizing.

Although the miracle of the bones could only be affected by the divine power, God desired the prophetic utterance of a human vessel. As Ezekiel prophesied to the bones, supernatural breath came into them. This breath brought life and mobilized them. This is what the gospel proclamation is all about—speaking life into those who are without life. This scene gives us a picture of prophetic evangelism and the impact that awaits a new breed of Spirit-led harvesting.

North America has seen two great awakenings in its history. In both time periods the spiritual landscape, which preceded each move of God, was dark, bleak, and unpromising. In each great awakening, God raised up Ezekiels—His mouthpieces to call the dead to life and prophesy a redemptive wind into being. I am convinced that there will be a third great awakening that will see a staggering number of souls come into the kingdom!

One thing is for sure: We must step into what Ezekiel stepped into—the critical arena of human need—armed with an obedient heart and the lifegiving Word of the Lord.

This book is written for several reasons. First, I want to impress that the prophetic proclamation of the gospel is the only hope for delivering a fallen planet to Christ. You and I have been given the Spirit of God, the Word of God, and His heart to be effective in reaching the lost. This book will prayerfully grip your heart and conscience with a fresh faith and burden to harvest.

Second, I want to submit some unique insights and effective means that you can use to reach hearts and proclaim the gospel in modern culture. Although I'm not advocating a programmatic approach to evangelism, there are some definite principles that are shared along the way. Being led of the Spirit defies mere methodology, yet there are some practical methods that are essential.

Third, I'm advocating a new synergistic blending of God's giftings—prophecy and evangelism—to break through modern resistances and the demonic walls that have been erected.

The chapters in this book are designed to cultivate a new hunger for the God-dimension to be released through you with miraculous manifestations to present the kingdom. Jesus said, "This gospel of the kingdom will be preached in all the world as a witness to all the nations, and then the end will come" (Matt. 24:14). This "gospel of the kingdom" requires a specific yielding on the part of the believer to play a significant role in human history and God's ultimate purposes. So join in the adventure.

A PROPHETIC IMPRESSION

I strongly sense a burden from the Lord for my nation in this time. I sense the Lord instructing believers to rise up in this hour. Events have transpired on a national scene that should have awakened a deeper sensibility within us towards God's eternal desire to gather in His harvest. Even in this time, we have a window of opportunity where the "Captain of our salvation" has gone before us to prepare hearts. The harvest is ripe and ready to be gathered now before that opportunity passes.

The opportunity of a lifetime must be seized during the lifetime of the opportunity. This window has a time constraint where negligence on our part would be disastrous to the destinies of multitudes. If this opportunity is not seized, we must live with the consequences of our inactivity, or with the fruit of our disobedience. God is patient toward us, not willing for any to perish, but for the grace of repentance to be received by the multitudes. You and I must take our turn in history and fulfill our call to be reapers and weepers, seeing someone's eternal address change forever.

This is an hour when God will give nations to those who will rise up and speak what the Spirit is saying, and not be afraid to get their hands dirty. Positioning and petitioning will be the key to unlocking the hearts of a generation in this last hour.

With each chapter, you will acquire the tools that are necessary to fulfill your assignment. You will be empowered to take action!

Chapter 1

Out of the Box

I CAN REMEMBER THE FIRST TIME that I stood on an Olympic-height diving board before what seemed like an ocean and a watery grave. Considering the fact that I didn't like heights, could only do the "dog paddle," and that it was my first time on a serious diving board, I froze and didn't want to go down. I remained where I was, pretending like I was still considering the jump. With jeers of complaints coming from those on the ladder behind me, I was stuck.

In some ways this is a depiction of the modern-day Church. We seem frozen over the pool waters of modern culture. We appear to be afraid of leaving the safety of the edge of our platforms to engage and spring into the mainstream of society, the exact flow that God has uniquely positioned for us to move into. You and I happen to have been born at an "edge" in history, where we see the ending of one epoch and the turned page of another. Right now, some people are wishing that they could go back in the line, but this transition zone will not be kind to that mentality.

Meanwhile, there are many others behind us in line on the diving board ready to jump into the human pool of felt needs and spiritual thirsts for wrong motives and causes. The choice is either to jump on our opportunity or go back to the end of the line and risk missing our turn in human history.

When you're not jumping on your turn, people are witnessing your vacillation and vegetation. Sometimes it's not the criticism or apparent failure that hurts you, but the feeling that you are not taken seriously and do not belong.

MAKING HISTORY OR BECOMING HISTORY

Jesus said in Matthew 5:13, "But if the salt loses its flavor...it is then good for nothing but to be thrown out and trampled underfoot by men." The phrase "losing its flavor" has the literal meaning of making them passive, or making them foolish. The original also implies that the consequence of not having impact is that our brand of Christianity will be treated with insulting neglect. The gifting God has bestowed upon us will either be disciplined or dissipated.

The modern-day "trampling" is highly chronicled. There have been massive attempts to take Christian concepts and faith off the cultural wall of human consciousness. You can't officially pray in schools or at college graduations. You can't have the Ten Commandments on government property or public property. Despite the alarming nature of such prohibitions, the most frightening aspect of all is that you and I might remain standing at the edge of the platform and never dive into our destiny! Failure to launch and engage will only make us accomplices to the crime of our generation.

As it turned out, I jumped—albeit somewhat awkwardly—but I jumped! I was never the same after the impact...and I have a feeling that you won't be either.

SURVIVAL OF THE FASTEST

Most of us feel, at least on occasion, that we are losing control. The rate of change today is unprecedented and we look somewhat unprepared for this change curve we're currently riding. In the fast-paced life of postmodern culture everything takes place in a New York City taxicab moment. It is like "survival of the fastest" or something.

We live in an "anything can happen and probably will" world. We're a culture heading somewhere we are not sure of, at breakneck speed. The unthinkable has become the acceptable; recycled opinions are passed as original thinking; and people settle for what is, rather than fighting for what could be. There are current cultural shifts, which means that our ministry must shift as well. To be effective in soul winning, one must be open to change.

People love progress. Technology is changing; medical fields are changing; people are thinking differently. Environments void of change or transformations are eventually void of vitality. It has been said, "Leadership is the ability to turn on a dime in a new direction." We need to drop the dime soon.

LIFE IN A BOX

An American illusionist/magician spent 44 days in a clear glass box (7 x 7 x 3 feet) suspended over London's Thames River. He left the box disheveled and sobbing: "This has been the most important day of my life." This revelation could be more important than you initially realize. His release from the box is an illustration for the Body of Christ. This chapter is about identifying and taking apart barriers—worn out models of evangelism.

In our world today, too many fear stepping out into a new opportunity more than they fear missing out on a new opportunity. The longer you tolerate something, the longer it dictates your experience.

It is known that you will never change your belief system until you acknowledge that it is the reason for your present situations. In order to change, one has to abandon all confining safety zones.

Life is not about staying in the safe places. Even Peter stepped out of the boat, despite the fact that the other disciples stayed on board. Peter found the motivation to step out and meet with the Author of life. *We* need to rediscover our cause, which releases forward momentum. Like Erwin McManus says, "The real tragedy is not that churches are dying but that churches have lost their reason to live!" We need to dial back into our cause again. A cause is what differentiates a hero from a lunatic.

ESCAPING THE LAND OF IRRELEVANCY

Darkness wants to keep us contained in the land of irrelevancy where we're busy doing what doesn't work, where it doesn't matter anyway. Diminished results and ever increasing pressures to produce have become the order of the day. How do you measure a healthy Christian meeting or a successful church? It has to go beyond the weekly body count or how many attended our last conference. These have their place, but must not unseat the dynamic of reaching the unchurched.

For decades the Church was where people looked for spiritual truth and answers to life and morality. Now we are experiencing a rude awakening where the Church is facing everything from jaded indifference to open hostility that our culture now demonstrates. We have to make the shift from just accommodating weekly Christian programs to empowering an army of believers to take their place and harvest in mainstream society. The chief goal of this hour must be to produce Christians who are not living for the next thrill, but are looking to take the next piece of enemy territory!

A NEWLY DEFINED FOLLOWER

Writer Michael Simpson is right when he said, "I believe that Christ being less attractive…is a by-product of a diluted Christianity." We must watch and rethink some of the Christian labels we use until we recognize a person's preconceived notion about Christianity. No doubt, certain terms have become more toxic than redemptive to our postmodern culture. My friend, Mike Bickle, says, "God is going to change the understanding and expression of Christianity in one generation." This statement is profound in that it includes change in both the way Christianity is going to be lived and the way it is going to be perceived.

An awakening will result when a new breed of standard bearers rise up and redefine "normal."

We are eyeing a cycle of unraveling amongst this generation. With the sanctity of human life and basic sanity going out the window, we are seeing a downsizing of virtue and a dumbing down of "tolerance." There is now a bullying from political correctness and an unmerciful dictatorial culture we've seen emerge. The entire world is reeling under political, economic, and ecological crisis. Yet, the one crisis that will bring the most widespread devastation is the spiritual crisis. This is a time of great spiritual intensity.

In seasons of unraveling you have to want increase and enlargement enough to undergo the change required to acquire it. To be out of the box is to break through the barriers to change.

I believe that you and I can no longer postpone, avoid, or resist change because staying the same will hurt us more than the cost of conducting our lives differently. We must change to prevent the dreaded alternative: culture and endtimes happening to us, instead of us happening to our end-time culture.

"Sing, O barren, You who have not borne! *Break forth into singing, and cry aloud, You who have not labored with child! For more are the children of the desolate Than the children of the married woman," says the Lord* (Isaiah 54:1).

God has the power to change your current circumstances. You may be barren now. You may not be productive now, but wait just a minute. With the power of the Holy Ghost, your life could break wide open!

Some seasons are seemingly filled with desolation, but take comfort in knowing that every season has a time frame and a divine seed. There's more available to us in the heavenlies than what we've currently apprehended. God is alerting you and I to raise our expectancy. Our expectancy will become our spiritual currency to allow transactions with Heaven. Be a risk-taker, not an undertaker.

I'm convinced that Jesus Christ died for you and I to be able to experience far more than what we've experienced thus far in life. We can become so much more than whatever it is we've currently become.

CONFINEMENT

I believe it's time for you and I (and the Body of Christ) to take the lid off our vessel and let the treasure out. Satan works overtime to keep us in the box and the confinement issue is one of satan's most powerful and effective strategies. He is satisfied to keep you confined; to keep you where you are at, and to prevent you from going where God wants to take you.

The Definition of Confinement:

1. Something that encloses, as borders or walls,
2. Something that restrains or holds back from movement, and
3. Something that places limits.

The opposite of confinement is movement. The early Church "moved." In moving, something or someone must be left behind. The enemy's confinement has been successful because it's subtle.

A confined believer loses victory. Confined Christians are actually a contradiction to their message: "Come to Christ; He'll set you free," when everyone can see they are trapped in boxes themselves.

Victory Is Defined As:

1. The overcoming of an enemy,
2. The achievement of mastery or success in struggle, or
3. An endeavor against odds or difficulties.

When we fail to contend with those things that hold us back, we also fail to develop "mastery" in areas that God desires to grow us in. We can't fight all our battles from the view of the pew. At some point we've got to go to the enemy's camp.

The overcomer in you rises up when you step out of your comfort zone. You must not abort or miscarry what the Holy Spirit desires to birth in you.

A confined believer loses value. They have perhaps developed an over-infatuation with what God once accomplished in their past. When I say "over-infatuation," I mean they are so enamored by that past thing, they're not growing up in the Lord to be able to cross the line satan has drawn in the sand.

When we choose to fight, to expand, we increase the "property value" of our faith. What you battle for becomes more prized in your eyes; as it is more prized by you, it will also be valued more by those who are watching you as well. No one takes a severely limited recluse seriously; the currency of their philosophy bottoms out and they become a contradiction to their message.

A confined church loses validity. It has nothing to say to mainstream society or the community. It revolves in its programs, events, and weekly service structure, virtually ignoring the unsaved outside its doors. A confined church is an expiring church, instead of an explosive church. Validity speaks of being at once relevant and meaningful. These are two terms that must make a comeback in modern Christianity.

Satan wants to get us "cocooning" instead of breaking his grip upon this generation. The second greatest punishment (after death) a prisoner can have, is solitary confinement, being shut off from the world around them. It doesn't matter if you have the pictures of the last supper or crosses on the wall—you are still alone. After a while, people in solitary confinement get drowsy and phase out mentally; their awareness becomes incapacitated.

Your enemy wants to subdue your awareness and release a slumbering spirit. In this state he can sell you on giving in to a comfortable life thereby causing a corpse-like complacency. You will always avoid the challenges of breaking out of the box into the maximum life that Jesus died to get you into.

The phrase "out of the box" simply means that someone or something has broken out from its barriers. It also means that someone has outgrown their history and has gone beyond their limitations.

ORIGINAL PACKAGING

Contemporary marketing and packaging has one problem: Almost everything you buy is so tightly fitted into its package that once you take it out, you can't get it back in! Have you ever been standing in Wal-Mart and opened a new package of T-shirts just to check the size for your child? We all know that as soon as it bursts out of that little plastic wrapper you're in trouble if you try to fold it up and put it back in to look any good.

There's a spiritual principle here. Once you bust out of where you've been confined, it is impossible to get you to conform back to your original dimension. And guess what? Satan knows it, and it's time for you and I to know it. He's afraid that you and I are going to bust out and never go back to the way we were.

Making Bones About Comfort Zones

Many believers allow themselves to stay in comfort zones, but the anointing comes to people who are willing to step out of their comfort zone. The fruit comes when the boundaries are crossed because that's where the anointing for growth lives.

We mistakenly think that the perimeter of our comfort zones protect us from hurt or fear. But that area is not about protection; it is really a demonic wall of confinement like the bars of a jail cell keeping us inside. Sometimes we allow confinement. We talk about what the devil has taken away from us, but more often than not, it's what we have given away.

Author Rick Richardson says, "When we start to make witnessing a passion and a priority we run into a major barrier: our 'boxes,' mental models of evangelism that keep us from pouring our passion into new ways of witnessing."

HOW TO GET OUT OF THE BOX

1. Collaborate with the Creator—The first step to getting out of the box is to fellowship with the God of the breakthrough. The apostle Paul got alone with God for his initial revelation that broke "Pharisaism" off of him. The Holy Spirit will charge you with fresh vision and boldness. God can replace the "is" with the "can be."

2. Let go of defensiveness—We have to yield to the newness that God releases in our spirits. We can't fight this divine process with comfort zone rationalizations. Once we let go, He lets go. T.D. Jakes, a great pastor and author, once said, "Only those who are willing to be stretched beyond the ordinary toward the extraordinary achieve their dreams."

3. Tackle the monster (traditions of man)—There are many human traditions that are not based on eternal principles. We must break the pattern that ties us to man-made mechanisms that get in the way of God's spontaneous illumination. Tackling this monster ensures that nothing will nullify the Word of God.

4. Seize the day—Realize that transitions can test our resolve. The will to change must be strong. Our will is like a muscle that strengthens with use. God will place resiliency and grace in our hearts.

5. Forever be a Student—Never marry a form or method again. The ability to keep a learning posture will be key to the prophetic evangelist. We must keep Jesus' yoke of discipleship upon us for life. A major mistake is to conclude that everything one knows at the moment is all that there is to know about a particular subject.

STRETCH OUT

Enlarge the place of your tent, and let them stretch out the curtains of your dwellings; do not spare; lengthen your cords, and strengthen your stakes (Isaiah 54:2).

We tend to want to enlarge, but we don't want to be stretched. You can't grow or expand without being stretched. Flexibility and the capacity to extend and amplify will be the prized commodity in the new millennium.

The greatest blessing God can entrust you with is when He can put you into a position where He can stretch you! If you feel that you're in over your head, you're in a God zone. God is going to get you in over your head to get a resource into you that is over your head.

The moment you get over your head, don't worry—don't get shook up, just look up, because God is about to come through!

It's like the butterfly that struggles and struggles, finally breaking out of his cocoon; God wants us to fight and break out of the perimeters of our boxes. It is at this point that we can go from crawling to soaring. He wants us to wrestle a little bit. He wants us to get in a place of prayer. Fight the enemy by speaking the Word, "Greater is He who is in me than he who is in the world"! Break free from your limitations! Break out of your religious thinking! Break free from your history! The enemy wants to use things that you're currently going through to bring confinement. You must remember that the ceiling you're up against today will be the floor you're going to stand on tomorrow.

33

RADICAL RECALIBRATION

What we need is a radical recalibration—a divine, precise adjustment for the particular function of impacting our generation for Christ. Real spirituality is birthed out of being current with the "now" move of God. Holy realignments will be necessary from time to time. Responding with shallow cosmetic changes will not only cause a loss of influence, but will become an attitudinal concession across the board.

A serious condition calls for a serious remedy; a new world calls for a new Church. Meaningful change is never a walk in the park. Sometimes reality can cause you to hit the ground face down, but to take the ostrich approach can make you an accessory to the crime.

Radical recalibration is what Peter did after fishing all night and coming back empty-handed (see Luke 5:1-6). Picture the frustration etched on Peter's face and the stress of falling behind in his business quota. Then Jesus told Peter to go out deeper and drop his nets again.

Peter probably pulled a muscle in his brain trying to justify this command. Sometimes your brain can be your biggest enemy. Peter knew the tendencies of fish and the normal patterns in the art of fishing, yet he knew he had to recalibrate to the mechanism of the wisdom of the Spirit. His response was classic as he said, "Nevertheless, at Your word, I will let down the net." The phrase "at Your word" represents a radical recalibration, one that we must all make to partake of the great catch of the endtimes. I'm sure from that point on Peter learned to live by divine inside information.

Mary, the mother of Jesus, demonstrated this principle when she encountered the messenger of the Lord. The angel said something was going to happen to her that was really outside her box! For that matter, it was outside the box of historical precedence and the biological laws of reproduction. The angel told of her forthcoming supernatural pregnancy and her birthing of the Savior. She was a teenager and engaged to Joseph, who could have chosen not to be so understanding, yet she made the radical recalibration. She boldly, yet submissively, stated, "Let it be done according to Your word."

It would have been immediately and historically ruinous for either of them to fail to recalibrate. George Barna says, "I've concluded that

34

within the next few years, America will experience one of two outcomes: either massive spiritual revival or total moral anarchy." The outcome will be contingent upon whether we radically recalibrate or radically recede.

Our challenge will be to get extravagantly in sync with God. I believe God is going to reshape His Church in glory and influence by bringing a radical recalibration to you and me. Before anyone or anything changes there must first be a high sense of urgency established. A visible crisis seems to do the trick, which is the way Jesus wants us to perceive our world.

The other pivotal ingredient is vision. Vision always plays a key role in aligning and inspiring actions in the human heart. The hallway to spiritual outbreak is divine desperation. Whatever it takes, you and I must become desperate. When desperation takes its place in our hearts, we no longer permit obstacles to block us.

The Genesis of Desperation

If you look at many of the patriarchs of the Bible, many of their wives were barren. It's interesting to note that as they took steps of faith, the barrenness was broken. Hannah, in First Samuel chapter 1, was barren. The Lord had literally shut her womb.

The Old Testament was written to provide examples for us; there is something behind the obvious to be grasped by the hungry. Hannah's rival, Peninah, severely provoked her. She was a baby-making machine. Elkanah had two wives and Peninah was the one who was making him a daddy over and over again.

I'm convinced God used Peninah's heightened fertility to draw something out of Hannah. This provocation becomes God's signature move to detonate desire inside of His vessels. I believe that we are seeing events happen in our nation to purposely provoke you and me as believers. It's almost as if the Lord intends that these things around us should provoke us into greater fruitfulness.

Through the provocation of someone else being fruitful, something else was being birthed in Hannah. She didn't quit and throw in the towel; she was being provoked to a place of intercession. She began to cry out to God by spending time at the temple becoming intimate with God. He was breaking the barrenness in her through her intimacy with the Holy Spirit, her intimacy in prayer. We all know the story: Hannah birthed one of the greatest of the prophets, Samuel, of whom it was said, "None of his words fell to the ground." Bottom line: if there is no desperation, then there will be no covenant, no intimacy, no fruit, and no relief from barrenness.

SPIRITUAL BARRENNESS

Years ago when I got saved, God birthed in me a desire to witness. This hunger developed into desperation to help change people's eternal address. The birthing of this dynamic in my life saved me from a nominal Christian existence with watered-down desires. We would be making a serious mistake if we were content with the growth we had already attained and had little ambition to reach the lost.

You possess what a fallen world desperately lacks. You can go beyond the familiar; you can defy the boundaries. You can go beyond what you've always been accustomed to doing; you can go beyond your groove. God made you to make a difference in your world, your marketplace, and your social networks. Draw on the resurrected One, who lives inside of you. I believe God is waking up the Church. It is a matter of a sleeping giant arising to the place of a greater impact in the nation that we live. We're going to go from hibernation to every nation. God is doing great things, and He is inviting us to be a part of it!

A GENERATION BIRTHED RIGHT

Hannah had to give birth to the prophet Samuel. He was the one to bring a new order, reforming the temple protocol from corruption to correction. Eli was becoming dull (see 1 Sam. 3:3). The lamp of God was flickering low and about to go out, but it didn't disturb him (yes, it was still burning, but things were not as they should be). We need God to bring on a new generation of Samuels—a generation that is prophetically keen and speaks words that pierce the armor of a hardened culture. Every generation is a step toward the fulfillment of God's eternal purposes. No matter what generation you were born in, you've been told you're in the problem generation. You are not a problem; you are another prophetic installment in the purposes of God.

One thing that I know for sure is that the immediate destiny of the nations can be found in the spiritual treasure chest of a new convert from this present generation. As the modern Church, we must align ourselves with God's purposes so that the spiritual babies born on our watch are birthed right and are raised up in a spiritually healthy environment.

Every generation presents the Church with a fresh, redemptive challenge. The methods of getting the gospel out changes, but the message never changes. Jesus' approach was different from person to person. He talked in terms that people could relate to. The methods from the past may not be effective today, but we must not fail to preach this timeless message, unchanged, in changing times. This matchless message is tied into a historic release of the glory of God in the earth. God will honor His promise to cover the earth with the knowledge of His glory. There's going to come a place in time where God is going to exalt the glory of the Lord on His people. It's going to be attractive. There's an evangelistic spirit of attraction that will happen before you even say anything.

REFUSING TO BE BOUGHT OFF

The story of Hannah perfectly illustrates a principle for the Christian who wants to break out of barrenness. Elkanah made two distinct attempts to appease his wife who was reproductively blocked. He gave her more blessings and said to her, "Am I not better to you than ten sons?"

The turning point for her becoming a mom and seeing the prophet Samuel's birth was found in a two-step resolve that she had made. First of all, she refused to settle for less or capitulate to "double portion" gifts that could have taken the edge off of her desire to break barrenness. The first attempt of buying off Hannah's resolve with "more blessings" represents the trap of the temptation of wanting God's gifts more than you see the need to plant God's gift of life in a lost person's heart. It is so easy to get caught up in distractions, or things that are blessings in their proper context, but can disconnect you from holy desperation to birth souls into the kingdom. Hannah broke through barrenness by not succumbing to the "bless me club" diversion.

The next trap was more challenging because it seemed more rational. The "Am I not better to you than ten sons?" proposition. This is reflected when Christians release themselves from the Great Commission because they "gave more in the offering this week" or "I'm going on a week of missions next summer" or "I'm in a Wednesday night discipleship group." All of these things are great, but you must not allow them to remove your urgency for souls. Hannah took these overtures from Elkanah in stride and remained in a place of desperation. Today, God is raising up a prophetic postmodern harvester who will not sell out to cultural or religious acquisitions or accomplishments short of advancing the kingdom of God in the hearts of humanity.

Desperation is so crucial to breaking out. Military oppressors and tyrants have found that once people get totally desperate, there is no maintaining their captivity, once this dynamic is in place.

Desperation has four stages:

1. Awareness

The first stage of desperation is where you first realize that something is missing. This stage hardly ever moves anyone to real action or change. Many people are aware of things that need fixing or alleviating. The problem with this stage is that it is not uncomfortable enough to get you to do anything differently. We must be convinced at a much deeper level that something needs to change. This stage is important because until this deficit comes to our attention, we can't do anything about it.

2. Embarrassment

The second stage of desperation is where we actually register a slight negative feeling about our deficit, but only at times. Usually it is only when we are concerned about our reputations around particular people, or when this feeling stings us in certain situations from time to time. The shame levels don't rise up high enough or often enough to produce the drive to do whatever it takes to change. This mentality is needed to negotiate the friction to turn things around.

3. Frustration

The third stage of desperation is where a nagging and foreboding sense rides you fairly consistently. Even without others highlighting our lack, we feel the pain—even if it is still somewhat bearable. This is the part where an intense distressing begins to grow in us. Many people rounding the last corner to permanent change or growth get here and stop without crossing the goal line. A.W. Tozer once said, "If you feel that where you are at is where you ought to be, you will remain where you are at." The next stage is the most crucial step in the entire process.

4. Intolerability

The final stage of desperation is the ultimate catalyst and the point of no return. This is where urgency and inner gravity releases momentous change. Desperation finally stamps within an individual a power and purpose that refuses to be denied. We need to recover this important level of conviction called desperation.

Hannah went to this level of desperation when she wept, prayed, and fasted before the temple continuously, culminating in a vow before the Lord. Desperation, as seen in Hannah, releases fresh intimacy, inspiration, and much needed impact. Great spiritual movements and revivals have been embarked upon because a core got to this point. I feel that the time we live in dictates that we must get intolerably desperate to become used by God.

You must realize that change will not occur unless a high enough sense of urgency is established. As long as your complacency level is high you won't produce or achieve your objectives. Without desperation, people won't give the extra effort that is essential to change; they won't make the needed sacrifices. They will cling to the status quo. One of the greatest gifts that God can release over a believer or nation is divine desperation. It becomes the impetus for dramatic metamorphosis.

A TIME FOR COVENANT

The final component that was integral to Hannah's breaking barrenness was the covenant she made with God. In First Samuel 1, Hannah made a covenant with the Lord that if He broke her barrenness with a son, she would give him back as a Nazarite unto the Lord.

A covenant is the agreement between two parties within the context of relationship, whereby a sacrifice and benefit is transacted. It is a binding promise that allows legal right of entry and the partaking of what one has.

The purpose of a covenant is to ensure faithfulness and commitment to one another. The covenant is actually a set of words that are spoken to define the nature of a relationship and set forth the principles of commitment to it. A covenant is something to be remembered. The Bible says "the Lord remembered her," demonstrating the respect God places on covenants.

We are saved by a covenant; we are joined to God's promises by a covenant. In fact we are given grace to achieve the purposes of God by covenant.

Bill Bright, the founder of Campus Crusade for Christ, began his ministry at one university and then it grew to 191 countries. His Four Spiritual Laws tract and the Jesus film have definitely impacted eternity for many people. He was an amazing leader who, along with Billy Graham, helped energize America's evangelical movement after World War II.

In 1950, Bright and his wife signed a covenant with God, literally relinquishing themselves and everything they owned to God. It was upon this amazing act that God birthed the vision for Campus Crusade within Dr. Bright. He once said, "I am convinced that had there been no contract, there would be no vision." He wrote the covenant out as a young man and signed his name at the bottom. It read, "From this day forward, I am a slave of Jesus Christ."

I can totally relate to this. Upon my conversion on the college campus, I stated before God that if He would reveal Himself to me, I would give Him everything in return and hold nothing back. I was tested in this many times. My call came as a result of this "holy moment" before

God. I had entered into a personal covenant with the Lord, before I even knew fully what it would release. John 12:24 portrays this phenomenal dynamic, which says that as we die to our own agenda and self-absorption we will be reapers of the harvest in greater measure.

Are you ready to enter into a great fruitfulness? Then enter into a covenant to sacrifice according to God's Word.

CHAPTER 2

CRAZY LOVE

IT WAS PROBABLY IN 1994 that my wife and I were directed by God to go to a particular conference. Between the main sessions, people who were in full-time ministry were invited to a luncheon where there were several prophetic ministers. As I was looking around, suddenly one of the speakers looked at me and said, "Sir, would you stand up?" I stood up and the first thing that came out of his mouth was, "If it wasn't for God's intervention between the ages of eight and ten, we would not be having this moment right now."

In that moment, I gasped, because at the age of nine, after my dad's death, I was diagnosed as having an enlarged heart. The doctor had said to my mom that they had to put a pacemaker in my chest or I might not make it. My mom walked out of the hospital in Berkeley, California, and looked up at the sky and pleaded, "Oh, God, please don't take my baby. Heal my son." We went to another specialist and—boom! He said I didn't have an enlarged heart! God heard my mother's cry for her only child.

The prophetic man went on to say other things about the direction that my wife and I would be taking soon after that. But then he said, "God shows me that you're a man of unusual passions. You have an enlarged heart (which, of course was a total play on the earlier word) in the spirit, because God has filled you with passions."

43

In that moment, I was feeling God all around me! I was shaking. He went on to say that not everyone would understand the unusual passions that God had given me, and boy, was he right!

THE CATALYST OF PASSION

The hunger for passion is universal. God designed the human soul to be passionate, abandoned, and fiery. Passion is a compelling emotion; it is a strong desire for something. Passion is a powerful catalyst. It acts like a magnet that attracts its keeper to its source.

Passionate people get things done and seem to be able to acquire the resources necessary to accomplish great undertakings. Passion is born out of commitment—the more of yourself that you offer to God, the more passion you'll receive in return. Passion overflows boundaries; it is not often logical or seemingly appropriate. To enter the world of passion we must relinquish our need to predict the outcome. Passion is what happens when we let go of control.

This kind of extreme passion I have titled, "crazy love." Crazy love puts you on the cutting edge because it is willing to bear the stigma of a new move of God. Crazy love has the components of both compelling passion and the willingness to abandon all. I believe that right now we are living in a time that demands crazy love.

THE ANATOMY OF CRAZY LOVE

I have found that God releases a pleasure in my soul through crazy love. I can sense the smile of God in my heart when I am consumed with this dynamic. There is a spiritual intensity found in this gift that disrupts our lives, status quo, and typical spiritual growth.

I'd like to make it clear that when I'm talking about crazy love, I'm not talking about shallow sentimentalism, nor am I talking about dumbing down to a religious mentality. I'm talking about a baptism of holy affection. I'm talking about the "first love" fervency that Jesus referred to in the Book of Revelation.

God is saying we're to lavish this love, break the jar, and release a fragrant love, a crazy love, about who God is (see Mark 14:3). A passion for Jesus and His eternal purposes must consume us. I'm convinced that we're living in a critical moment in time. God is imparting divine abandonment that will appear fanatical to those who don't understand you.

A revival of intimate encounters with God is coming, and as a result, believers will be filled with extravagant fervency.

For Zion's sake I will not hold My peace,
And for Jerusalem's sake I will not rest,
Until her righteousness goes forth as brightness,
And her salvation as a lamp that burns.
The Gentiles shall see your righteousness,
And all kings your glory (Isaiah 62:1-2a).

This passage speaks prophetically about God giving us an enlarged heart. There will be an overflow of passion culminating in a phenomenal worldwide witness. The key will be that which burns in us.

Isaiah is saying that God is going to be relentless on you until:

1. A new standard of Christianity is reflected, and a blazing righteousness goes forth like a nuclear power plant explosion. This speaks of a global witness that sees a supernova revelation of the glory in its brilliance shining through you.

2. A passionate, holy zeal violently consumes you with an unparalleled inner fire. This speaks of an internal, supernatural fire, a spirit of burning that flows within you in an unhindered fashion.

CRAZY PAUL

Let's look in the Book of Acts where Paul is standing in front of King Agrippa, a man with the power to give him the thumbs up or thumbs down.

Now as he thus made his defense, Festus said with a loud voice,
"Paul, you are beside yourself! Much learning is driving you
mad!" But he said, "I am not mad, most noble Festus, but speak
the words of truth and reason" (Acts 26:24-25).

The words "beside yourself" mean to rave as a maniac, and it's the idea of incessant craving. What he was saying was that Paul was positively "mental." He thought he had lost it and was raving like a maniac, certifiable, living *la vida loca*. Festus accused him of being crazy.

Revival is about being extreme. Extreme is going well beyond the ordinary or the average.

Actor Denzel Washington has this one line in a movie that puts fear into the heart of his adversary. He says, "There's something strangely liberating about going crazy."

Modern culture is not drawn to Christianity because the little they are exposed to is not extreme enough for them. I'm not talking about being a fool, but I think the world really wants to see a Christian who is totally enthralled with who Jesus is.

ROMANCE AND REFORMERS

I remember when I first began to feel like God was speaking to me about my wife, Barbara. She would leave a message on my answering machine. I would play that thing over and over! I forgot to eat at times. I felt intoxicated. The grass was green, the hills were alive, the skies were blue—I was in the *Sound of Music*. And all she did was leave a message on my answering machine!

We need a major dose of divine romance. Either you fall victim to the spirit of the age or you live on a higher plane. One of the great reformers, Francis Xavier, charged the apathetic European students of his day to "give up your small ambitions and come and preach the gospel of Christ."

BEING UNREASONABLE

Literary giant, George Bernard Shaw, is quoted to say, "The reasonable man adapts himself to the world. The unreasonable one persists in trying to adapt the world to himself. Therefore all progress depends upon the unreasonable man."

Reasonable people try to fit in; unreasonable people try to get other people to fit into God's plan. All progress is dependent upon the crazy lover.

Returning to Paul, Festus said, "What you've learned has driven you crazy." What have we to show for all of our learning? Our spiritual learning shouldn't be just systematic theology books, but a distinguishable crazy love that goes public. At first Paul denies it, but later on in

Second Corinthians 5:13 he basically says, "If I'm in my right mind, it's for your sake, but for God, I'm out of my mind."

GOING FANATICAL

Some years ago, I was in an airport in Denver. I was going to speak for a friend of mine. As I was getting off the plane, I saw two girls and a guy who were dressed in Eastern garb, soliciting people. The girl came toward me with this KFC-looking basket (without the Colonel on it). They were taking donations for the cult they were representing. She had pictures of the various times that they had gotten together as a cult group to worship this guru dude. She walked over to me and said, "I represent the Higher Consciousness of the 7th Nirvana Association. Have you heard of 'master so and so'?"

I said, "No, but can I tell you about my Master?"

I immediately jumped in and started telling her about Jesus. As I was sharing Jesus with her, she put her bucket underneath her arm and started listening. Her other coworker started listening to me too, as I explained how Jesus Christ had changed my life.

At this point there were still two girls and a guy. The guy must have been the leader, higher up in the hierarchy. He came over and I could see he was a little ticked. He was about to lose his converts, so he stepped boldly in front of them and said to me, "I know who you are. You, you, you're a fanatic. That's what you are, a fanatic! Fanatics are a dime a dozen." Then he grabbed the girls and walked away.

I stood there thinking to myself, "Okay, these people in the Denver Metropolis Airport who have a KFC bucket are wanting to tell me about their 'master so and so' and I'm the fanatic here? Hello, is anyone home?" Then I realized that the man's comment might have been the greatest compliment given to me because here is what I know about fanatics: Fanatics won't give up, let up, or shut up, until they get up, rise up, and take up all who Christ wants them to be!

David Du Plessis, known to many as Mr. Pentecost, said, "I'd rather tone down a fanatic than to try to raise the dead." If that is what a fanatic is, would to God that I would even be a greater fanatic! Even more so, that we would have a nation full of people that are just like that for Jesus Christ, because right now crazy love fanatics are too rare to be a dime a dozen.

> *"For the king, before whom I also speak freely, knows these things; for I am convinced that none of these things escapes his attention, since this thing was not done in a corner. King Agrippa, do you believe the prophets? I know that you do believe." Then Agrippa said to Paul, "You almost persuade me to become a Christian." And Paul said, "I would to God that not only you, but also all who hear me today, might become both almost and altogether such as I am, except for these chains"* (Acts 26:26-29).

FROM ALMOST TO ALTOGETHER

Today's church has given us a strain of Christianity that I would call "almost Christianity" masquerading as genuine Christianity. What is normal in terms of Christianity in our world today has so nose-dived that we need a group of people who will get some crazy love on them and redefine normal. God is calling us to go from nominal to phenomenal. How many of you know that almost is never good enough? You're in your dentist's office and he's drilling in your mouth. You look over on his wall and he has this certificate that says that he "almost passed his dental exam." How many of you know that's not good enough? The fuel that moves you from almost to altogether, in terms of commitment, is crazy love.

Without "crazy love" you'll never be able to speak freely to someone who will be antagonistic to the message of hope. One will never speak effectively until they can speak freely. Speaking powerfully and prophetically requires that you maintain an inner atmosphere of liberty. You have to be free of human pressures to flow with God's Spirit.

Crazy love allows you to challenge convention. When crazy love is upon an individual, he will be uninhibited in his expression of faith. Whenever I feel tight or nervous, it's hard to capture the flow of the Spirit or tap into the mind of Christ. When fear comes in, so does the adversary of our souls. Crazy love allows you to stand and flow in the Spirit.

PRISON BREAKING FROM PEOPLE-PLEASING

Before King Agrippa, Paul demonstrated that he had experienced a significant breakthrough. This same kind of breakthrough is a must for every prophetic evangelist. It is perhaps the most crucial battlefield because it affects one's ability to speak, discern, and flow in the gifts of the Spirit.

This enemy paralyzes and seeks to shut you down at every point. Its name is the spirit of rejection, and it manifests as the fear of man.

But rise and stand on your feet; for I have appeared to you for this purpose, to make you a minister and a witness both of the things which you have seen and of the things which I will yet reveal to you (Acts 26:16).

Paul knew that King Agrippa's dad (King Agrippa I) was responsible at that time for the execution of James, one of the 12 disciples. Who knew if dad and son had more in common than just their names? Yet Paul made sure the truth was on trial, rather than his personal safety or self-esteem. Like Paul, we must resist people-pleasing. I am convinced that once satan identifies this weakness in people, he uses it against them to keep them ineffective.

Fear of man has shut down many witnessing opportunities. It often causes us to say things that soften the blow of conviction. One of the greatest revivalists, Charles Finney, taught that in witnessing we work against the Holy Spirit when we try to make everybody feel happy all the time. Whenever we give in to fear we move away from our authority base that the Father has given us and furnished through His Word. Instead, Paul allowed crazy love to rise up within his heart, which freed him from insecurity and fear of man. Two of the greatest obstacles to being an effective witness are the spirit of rejection and the fear of man.

THE PEOPLE-PLEASING PATTERN

We're a culture built around seeking approval and people-pleasing. A definition of people-pleasing would be the tendency to cater to other's demands and preferences to the harm or violation of one's personal conviction or well-being.

Here are some irrational beliefs that people-pleasers are caught up in:

1. "I must be popular with everyone." No, everyone is not going to like you. People are fickle, and the rules change. It's important to say to yourself, "Hey, I'm going to be true to who and what God has made me to be, and my convictions."

2. "I must do nothing to cross other people." If you think you have to keep everyone happy, you are going to be disappointed. If they can't stay happy on their own, you're not going to make them happy. We can try to bless and encourage people, but the moment you feel responsible for making someone happy, you become a people-pleaser.

3. "If someone doesn't accept me, it must mean that I failed." Human rejection is nothing more than an expression of someone's opinion. One opinion should not dictate failure as it relates to my life. There are always going to be people who will have different opinions and different tastes. God has given us His approval, or extends His approval, to a life that honors Him. If we will honor God, God's validation supersedes anyone else's validation or approval of our lives.

Two downfalls of people-pleasing include:

1. You will be in a position where you will deny what you know to be true. Aside from the divine will and purpose of God's plan, did you know that it was the Pharisees who turned the crowd against Jesus? (On the other hand, there were some Pharisees who believed Jesus was Lord.) If we fail to stand with the truth, we lose the witness that is associated with it. Our alignment with truth will release conviction and captivate the attention of those whom we're trying to reach.

> *Nevertheless even among the rulers many believed in Him, but because of the Pharisees they did not confess Him, lest they should be put out of the synagogue; for they loved the praise of men more than the praise of God* (John 12:42-43).

There were rulers who looked in His eyes, they saw His miracles, they saw His life, and they said, "He's for real, but if we go along with Him, we'll be put out and they won't like what we say."

2. You will be in a position where you will make false concessions. You will no longer make a decision based on what is right or wrong, but

on the basis of who is around you. We recognize that as weakness. Remember Pilate? He wanted to let Jesus go because he knew that the Man was innocent, but he saw the angry crowd. He let public opinion prevail and forever made infamous the simple washing of hands. It affected his ability to make a right decision by letting a murderer be set free, and not the One who would set all men free.

Why do people give in to fear of man? God made us to want to please so that we would want to please Him. He made us to want to live our lives to give pleasure to the Creator. To know that you have the smile of God on your life means you can meet with other's frowns and it's okay.

Here's the key to break the squeeze: Remember the rewards of pleasing God. The Bible says pleasing God brings blessing. He's the same yesterday, today, and forever. His opinion of you is not going to change based on what some folks are saying about you this week. God knows us and He still chooses to love us! Once you have God's approval, who else is there to impress?

> But as we have been approved by God to be entrusted with the gospel, even so we speak, not as pleasing men, but God who tests our hearts. For neither at any time did we use flattering words, as you know, nor a cloak for covetousness—God is witness. Nor did we seek glory from men, either from you or from others, when we might have made demands as apostles of Christ (1 Thessalonians 2:4-6).

REJECTION: DARKNESS'S WEAPON OF CHOICE

Rejection has become satan's modern weapon of choice. Many would-be testimonies in the making have been short-circuited due to this wanna-be terrorist. Jesus gave us Heaven's remedy for earth's untouchables. He told them to "shake off the dust."

> Whatever city you enter, and they receive you, eat such things as are set before you. And heal the sick there, and say to them, "The kingdom of God has come near to you." But whatever city you enter, and they do not receive you, go out into its streets and say, "The very dust of your city which clings to us we wipe off

against you. Nevertheless, know this, that the kingdom of God has come near you" (Luke 10:8-11).

"Shake off the dust" means to release the rejection like a boxer slipping his opponent's punch, and keep attacking. Getting free from the spirit of rejection is as easy as shedding some unwanted dust. Don't let the devil shut you down with the threat of "dust." Brush off the threat of the disapproval of people and continue being a witness for Christ. You've been anointed by God to see miracles and do some dust busting! We've got to understand there's a battle. Don't let the residue of rejection cling to you. It's still worth it to witness, even if people reject you. Somebody's soul is worth any embarrassment that you may fear.

WHEN IT'S ALL ON THE LINE

Crazy love means that you're not going to stay in normal mode; you're not going to let the world's cultural wisdom squeeze you into its mold. Crazy love means the world's politically correct agenda can't dictate to you anymore.

It was September 15, 1999. There was a church in the southeast that had a "See You at the Pole" rally. At this rally, there were multiple churches that had gotten together with predominately youth, along with some parents and pastors. A man walked in on the rally with a gun. Someone yelled, "Get down!" The gunman shot the guy who had shouted and soon four others. Two were dead immediately and three were critically wounded.

As he was walking through the crowd with his gun, he said, "Your religion is blankety-blank." All of a sudden, one young man named Jeremiah stepped out. The moment the man spoke against Jesus Christ, this young man, Jeremiah, said, "No sir, it isn't."

Then the gunman walked right over to him and said, "What did you say?" and put his gun right up to his head. Jeremiah answered back to him, "What you need is Jesus Christ." As the gun was still on Jeremiah, he continued to say, "You can shoot me if you want. I know where I am going; I'm going to Heaven."

Jeremiah's youth pastor was on the ground grabbing his leg, as if to say, "Get down, get down!" All of a sudden, the youth pastor heard a loud shot. BAAAAMMM! He was fully expecting that Jeremiah would fall right there into his arms. He lifted up his head up, and what happened was tragic. The gunman took the gun off of Jeremiah and, sadly, used it on himself.

Here's the truth about this kid Jeremiah. This is astonishing. He had only recently given his heart to the Lord.

One hundred years ago the missionary statesmen, John R. Mott, prophesied, "The worldwide proclamation of the gospel awaits accomplishment by a generation which shall have the obedience, courage, and determination to attempt the task."

LIVELY COALS OR STONE COLD

And because lawlessness will abound, the love of many will grow cold (Matthew 24:12).

Satan wants you to become the temperature of the culture that surrounds you, a believer bound by a stone cold heart. The word *cold* means, "Reduction of temperature by evaporation." By exposure to hardness and darkness in the times that we live in, our love and passion will begin to cool by degrees.

It's a damaging process that finds genius in its subtlety and patience to evolve within an individual. It's a picture of what will happen over a period of time; it's not something that will happen overnight. When you see churches and individuals who do not have the energy to reach out, it's an indication that their love has grown cold.

In Numbers 16:37 (NAS), the Lord told Moses to, "Scatter the burning coals abroad." This is precisely what the Great Commission is all about—spreading the Word with a fiery heart.

A Message for a Medium

My wife and I had a campus ministry at a small university town in Northern California. I had a student with me who I had recently led to the Lord. We were driving down the street and went past a psychic's house that had a big picture of Jesus in the window. Everyone knew this woman psychic, who lived and worked right in the middle of town.

This new Christian said to me, "I guess she's a Christian, huh?" I said emphatically, "No way," and began to explain that the Bible says that psychic phenomena are considered to be an abomination by God. He pressed me further by asking, "Why, then, does she have a picture of Jesus in her window?"

I was disturbed that day because he had made a good point. I started praying and asking God why. It got to me because a picture of Jesus in a psychic parlor can deceive folks, and the devil wants to trip up people in any way he can. As I was praying, I felt like the Lord said, "I want you to go to 'Madam So-and-So's' psychic parlor. Here is the word I want you to bring to her: She has exactly one year to get right with Me, and if she doesn't do this in one year, she'll face some consequences."

"All right, God, You want me to go prophesy over a psychic." But I was obedient. In fact, the young man who I had been with even wrote her a letter imploring her to give her heart to Christ. We were thinking about putting the letter in the mail, but I felt God was telling me to go to her in person.

We went to her house, knocked on her door, and her daughter opened the door. I could see that she was in a séance or something in the next room. We told the daughter that we needed to see her mom and that it was very important, because we had a message for her. She asked, "Who is the message from?"

My friend and I looked at each other and we said, "God."

She said, "You guys are Christians, huh? We're Christians too. We go to a church."

I said, "Time out. No, you can't do that."

She said, "Oh, yeah, remember the three Magi? Well, they followed the stars to get to Jesus and it's all the same."

I said, "No, no, you need to read the whole story, girlfriend, because after they followed the stars to Jesus, they didn't follow the stars anymore; they followed the Creator of the stars. They didn't go back the same way they came. They got changed when they met Jesus!"

So the daughter was ticked, but she called her mom anyway. Madam So-and-So came to the door and she was "large and in charge." She was mad! I tried to tell her that the Lord loved her and He had sent His Son to die on a cross to get her free. I told her the demons she was

CRAZY LOVE

working with were going to eventually pickpocket her soul and send her to the same demise they were heading for.

She wasn't hearing it; she was angry. At that point, my friend handed her his letter, then I said, "The Lord said, 'You have one year to get your house in order, and if you don't get right in one year,' God says, 'that's it.'" What happened next in this woman's life we don't know; all we know is that we were obedient to the Lord.

IT'S WORTH THE STINK

Now David said on that day, "Whoever climbs up by way of the water shaft and defeats the Jebusites (the lame and the blind, who are hated by David's soul), he shall be chief and captain." Therefore they say, "The blind and the lame shall not come into the house" (2 Samuel 5:8).

We see David coming into an anointing that he's been promised for years. As he comes into this anointing, there's a task that is set before him. What he needs to do first is to overthrow the Jebusites and recapture Jerusalem. Can you imagine a time in Israel's history when they were not occupying the place of worship? Jerusalem, the city, was to them the epicenter of adoration, and it had been captured.

This is a picture of a Christian whose passions have somehow diminished because their love has been taken captive. David's first assignment with the anointing was that he had to overthrow the Jebusites and establish a place for God's presence. In order for David and the Israelites to enter into all the benefits of God's redemptive plan, they had to overturn these Jebusites. Now here's what happened. David discovered that the only way to get up into the city was to have someone go up through the gutter. He said to his men, "If you go up the gutter, I will make you chiefs and captains."

Do you know what goes on in the gutter? When I was in inner city Oakland, sometimes we would play by the gutter. It stunk. Rats were in there, and who knows what else.

Sometimes you've got to go through a gutter to get to your goal. Sometimes you have to hold your breath and go through some sewage to get your passion back. Sometimes discipline stinks. But if that's what

55

it takes to get your epicenter of adoration back, then so be it. We have got to have a place in our lives where we establish a time for the presence of God.

RECIPE FOR CRAZY LOVE

Crazy love begins when people encounter God. Paul encountered God in a big way when he fell off his horse and became blind. All of a sudden, in that very moment, something happened to Paul's heart.

He got up off of the ground, now defending all he had formerly persecuted, abandoning all he had clung to. The man went berserk for Jesus.

When I first responded to an altar call, God met me in an unusual way. He so prevailed upon me that I knew I would do whatever, and go wherever, to encounter His glory again. I had tunnel vision for God that my friends didn't understand.

Crazy love is fed through a fasted lifestyle. It is proven that what we sacrifice and suffer for is what we become most attached to. I see an emerging generation with a martyr mentality; believers who "love not their lives unto death."

Paul fasted his first weekend in the kingdom. (He even went without water.) No doubt, this fostered fervency in the man who the Holy Spirit inspired to write more than half of the New Testament.

The way we live is a reflection of the state of our hearts. Yet, the state of our hearts is enflamed by our lifestyles. We've seen the indulgent lifestyle cripple the spiritual passions of a generation of nominal believers. The more we can do without material and sensual things, the more we will partake of the spiritual delicacies that feed crazy love.

In Scripture, Nazarites were people of extreme devotion; they did not drink wine or eat grapes, which represented the pleasures of this life. Nazarites possessed a burning zeal for God and lived in radical abandonment with God. There's no coincidence here; they found the connection between a fasted lifestyle and crazy love passion.

Crazy love grows when you go out on a limb. Lately, I have been feeling that the Holy Spirit is leading me to go farther out a limb than at any other previous time. Sometimes, it is as if I can hear the snapping sound of the limb behind me, yet God always seems to come through. In fact, I'm convinced that we're seeing miracles that we wouldn't see if we hadn't stepped out in faith.

There's a spirit of faith that comes on a person as we step out in radical obedience that seems too "out there" for play-it-safe religionists. God is waiting to bless a generation on both ends—with crazy love faith and with miraculous outbreaks to possess the harvest.

Apostle Paul stayed out on a limb for God and explained that if he appeared safe and sane it was solely for the people. Yet, for God's sake, he was unsafe and insane, and stayed overextended in the faith realm. The "fallout effect" of crazy love passion was explosive on the apostle from Tarsus. By stepping out in faith, Paul's life was infectious on people who got around him: Timothy, Titus, Silas, and many others. Everywhere Paul went the reaction of his passion was evident in riots or revival breaking out; yet indifference certainly wasn't on the menu!

There are many things that we don't have control over, but we can control the passion and intensity with which we live our lives. To get the fruitful life that God has purposed for you, you must go out on a limb away from the ordinary and complacent.

David's men got through the gutter, and Jerusalem was restored, not to mention their new positions were definitely a bonus. Explosive passion and promotion awaits the crazy lover who will go the distance. In this next chapter we will visit the concept of adding the prophetic to our evangelism.

CHAPTER 3

WHEN PROPHECY MEETS EVANGELISM

I CAN REMEMBER A DAYTIME TALK SHOW some years ago. A certain spiritualist gave readings over the audience and took live callers. She was very upbeat and sounded positive, yet something sinister lurked beneath her self-help psychic sound bytes.

Later, it dawned on me what was going on. I had seen clairvoyance meet humanism and it was immediately popular and entrancing. Satan has always pushed the humanist manifesto gospel, but now it smacked of the counterfeit prophetic meeting a counterfeit gospel. We see this phenomenon in the explosion of the psychic hot lines, which is the mixture of horoscope and pop psychology. This combination is the mainstay of the New Age movement.

What would happen if we allowed the authentic to combine a message with miracles before a spiritually starved generation? We desperately need prophetic evangelism because an entire generation is at stake.

IT'S BEYOND US

How is this generation—engrossed by the supernatural—going to come to God? The solution is that we hold a part of the answer, but God holds the other part.

Conversion is a supernatural work. I can evangelize, but I cannot convert a soul. It is in the Holy Spirit's power alone to shine the light of revelation that leads a lost person to get saved. Yet many times people don't witness because they feel it's beyond them.

That is where prophetic evangelism has got to begin; we have to have a revelation. Prophetic evangelists don't rely on their abilities to persuade people; they rely on the Holy Spirit's ability to reveal. Our job is to share Christ and to follow the finger of God. If I do what God wants me to do, He'll bring the fruit.

THE TESTIMONY OF THE LORD

And to her it was granted to be arrayed in fine linen, clean and bright, for the fine linen is the righteous acts of the saints. Then he said to me, "Write: 'Blessed are those who are called to the marriage supper of the Lamb!' " And he said to me, "These are the true sayings of God." And I fell at his feet to worship him. But he said to me, "See that you do not do that! I am your fellow servant, and of your brethren who have the testimony of Jesus. Worship God! For the testimony of Jesus is the spirit of prophecy" (Revelation 19:8-10).

Many scholars believe that John is speaking to an angel, a specific angel. In fact, this angel's job description was to be Jesus' publicist in the Old Testament. Whenever there was a revelation about the Messiah, many scholars believe that this angel, who called himself "your fellow servant," gave the revelation. He would prophesy about the coming Messiah. Prophecy is history being declared in advance. Scholars believe that this angel gave prophecies to the various prophets: Isaiah, Ezekiel, and many others.

Prior to the birth of Jesus, this angel alone carried the "testimony of Jesus." Now the angel acknowledges that a baton had been passed to the Church to carry this testimony. This angel embodies the coming together of the prophetic and the evangelistic.

The phrase "the testimony of Jesus Christ is the spirit of prophecy" is important because it points to the fact that the testimony of Jesus Christ is the gospel. Second Timothy 1:8 says, "Do not be ashamed of the testimony of our Lord." The verse in Revelation indicates that there is a linking between the eternal purposes of these two anointings, the prophetic and the evangelistic. The testimony of the Lord Jesus Christ (the gospel) is equated to the Spirit of prophecy.

While I continue to contend for more of God's empowerment, I also believe that the moment I came to Christ, I had something to launch out with in witnessing. Whenever I set unnecessary preconditions, I deny myself a harvest. Prophecy is not just for the purpose of blessing discouraged Christians, or for being used inside the church house to jump-start a flat service. The prophetic is an anointing for revelatory release and a spiritual flow that we must contend for 24/7 and must be appropriated with both the churched and the unchurched. When a believer eagerly desires to prophesy, that individual is drawn into a greater fluency in prophetic giftings.

In Joel 2:24, the prophet speaks of a time when the threshing floor shall be "full of wheat," at the same time that the "vats shall overflow with new wine and oil." This passage is associating the prophetic with an abundance of souls. Joel goes on to tell us that the prophetic will bring insight, utterance, and inspiration. He says that a generation will prophesy and people will see visions and be given dreams.

Joel finishes chapter 2 by declaring that in the midst of all this prophetic activity, "Whoever calls on the name of the Lord shall be saved" (Joel 2:32). There is a back and forth interplay between prophecy and harvest to be noted in this passage.

The design of prophecy is to bear testimony to Jesus. It's not the only design, but it is the ultimate goal. It is like a picture of a wrestling tag team. Ecclesiastes 4:9-12 tells us that "two are better than one," for they will receive a better reward for their labors. It goes on to say that "one may be overpowered," but a "threefold cord is not quickly broken." When prophecy meets evangelism, a tag team is formed and the darkness that has blinded the minds of the unbelieving is defeated. We need the two to form a divine synergy to usher in the harvest.

Oxen Issues

Where no oxen are, the trough is clean; but much increase comes by the strength of an ox (Proverbs 14:4).

61

As Solomon accurately describes, there is a curious give and take dynamic when it comes to the oxen issue. This dynamic centers on a value system that every leader and soul winner must evaluate for themselves.

In early Jewish culture, an ox was equivalent to a tractor for a farmer. It would have severely hampered a Jewish family to be without their oxen. Today, our "oxen" for the kingdom is God's prophetic component in a church service. Without the oxen you have no mess and you have the bragging rights for the tidiest church service around. With the oxen you have a resource of strength, a promise of increase, and a church service promising some spontaneity.

Whenever the prophetic component is included, you will definitely face some messy "oxen issues." The unpredictability factor makes the people who would rather have everything programmed, nervous. You also have to deal with the growth in the fluency of the prophetic.

I have been faced with these issues in ministry over the years. Many times, particularly after those "messy" moments, I wondered if my life wouldn't be easier without the oxen. Typically, what would cure me of this hang-up would be a moment in a service where the oxen showed up. The fruit of the Holy Spirit that was given the freedom to reign was startling, contrasted to the approach of those services with "no deviation from the written program." I've learned to risk predictability and comfort zone security for miracles, Spirit-charged deviations, and unexpected harvest opportunities.

Despite the popular approach of some, we have a reality generation where unpredictability and spontaneity is attractive. In fact, the "messy" issue isn't as offensive (if handled with honesty and love) as it was a generation ago.

No one leaves our services talking about how clean our stables are, but rather, how strong our oxen are. Even a passing familiarity with Church history reveals that the oxen always brought exceptional increase, and the Church moved ahead in those times. Without the prophetic, our evangelistic programs suffer from the lack of strength to impact the unchurched. We will also miss the strong tangible presence of God that comes when the Holy Spirit is honored.

Proverbs 14:5 says, "A faithful witness does not lie." I can't consider myself honest if I hide the oxen from the audience. Our services must reflect His nature more than our own.

YOU ARE ONE OF THEM

Too often we've allowed the fear of messes and people's preferences to cause us to duck into a less than empowered witness.

One time I was speaking at a prophetic conference along with a minister, Dennis Cramer, who is gifted in the prophetic. He had just finished writing a book on prophecy. We were having a meal together on our way from the airport and I started thumbing through his book. All of a sudden, he points at me and says, "I wrote in my book about a new breed of prophetic evangelists, and you are one of them!" As he said it, I stopped eating and felt a "holy rush."

I didn't really know what to do with that because it was the first time I had ever heard of that term. In my own mind these were two separate camps. There was the prophetic camp and the evangelism camp. I would go to conferences where they would challenge you to go out and win souls; I felt like I was one of them. Then I would go to the prophetic conferences and they're prophesying and activating people; and I felt like one of them too. I would come back from those conferences feeling so schizophrenic. What am I?

I knew that I was called to be an evangelist, but I loved prophecy. One could get the impression that they were so distinct that there was no agreement between the two camps.

I began to have this strong stirring about the concept: What if prophecy met evangelism? The prophetic anointing is able to look into the heart of God and have the ability to discern the things that the enemy is trying to launch. The anointing of the evangelist has the ability to look into the heart of lost culture and see a need. What if the connection came together? How lethal could that be to the kingdom of darkness? What if in just one day we saw hundreds of thousands of people getting saved in major cities all across the United States and abroad?

What if we took full advantage of the synergy of joining prophecy and evangelism? What is synergy? Synergy is:

1. A mutually advantageous compatibility of distinct elements.
2. The working together of two things to produce an effect greater than the sum of their individual effects.

Acts 2 is a great example of this. Prophecy and evangelism were combined to release the Church's first great harvest. The disciples came out of the upper room speaking in a supernatural language, and Peter stands up and immediately quotes Joel: "This is what was spoken by the prophet Joel" (Acts 2:16). He immediately brings attention to the prophetic dimension here. Additionally, he says, "Save yourself from this perverse generation" (see Acts 2:40). (This is the essence of the gospel message.) Three thousand folks got saved through this connection to the writing of a prophet, Joel, combined with the message to "get saved."

AT YOUR WORD

When He had stopped speaking, He said to Simon, "Launch out into the deep and let down your nets for a catch." But Simon answered and said to Him, "Master, we have toiled all night and caught nothing; nevertheless at Your word I will let down the net." And when they had done this, they caught a great number of fish, and their net was breaking (Luke 5:4-6).

Let's look again at this passage. One night Peter goes out fishing. It's eerily silent as he catches nothing. He's disgruntled as he wonders how he is going to feed his family. Not only that, but he spent all night fishing when he could have slept if he had known he wouldn't catch anything.

Jesus says to him, "Launch out in the deep." Peter was an expert fisherman and could easily have resisted this directive, but instead says, "Nevertheless, at Your word, Lord." Peter could have kept doing his program, the same program that worked over and over again. But this time his well-trusted methods didn't work.

This is a picture of programmatic evangelism. We do the same thing, the same way every time, even though we're dealing with different situations. The carbon copy approach is the way a lot of evangelism has been taught.

What we need is a "nevertheless, at Your word" experience. What prophetic evangelism represents is "at Your word" evangelism. When Jesus said, "Launch out into the deep," Peter still had to let down his net. Jesus did not prophesy to the fish by saying, "Jump into the boat!" Neither is He telling the world to go to our Christian meetings. The Bible says we are to "go into all the world."

Peter had to throw out the net. But he threw it out where Jesus told him to throw it out. What happened next? There was such a big catch that their nets began to break! Can you imagine having so much fish that the boats began to sink? It was the greatest catch of Peter's life!

What does Jesus say to him? He basically said, "Up to this point you've been catching fish, but from now on you will be catching men." He was giving him a picture of prophetic evangelism.

Prophetic Sensitivity to the Seeker

But if all prophesy, and an unbeliever or an uninformed person comes in, he is convinced by all, he is convicted by all. And thus the secrets of his heart are revealed; and so, falling down on his face, he will worship God and report that God is truly among you (1 Corinthians 14:24-25).

Notice that it doesn't say, "If the prophets prophesy or if the unusually or highly-gifted prophesy." It says, "If all prophesy." This meant everyone in attendance at the Corinth church. Paul is saying that it is quite possible that every single person in the room has the potential to be used in the prophetic.

Many might say, "You don't want to prophesy if a first-time visitor comes in your church. What if they run out crying, "They're crazy in there! I'm just too sensitive and I can't stand it!" That's what we think sometimes.

First of all, I don't believe that the seeker is that easily offended anymore. They've been watching TV shows that are full of the supernatural; they've been reading paranormal books; and they've been watching reality-based séance shows. Yet we think they're going to be blown away when we speak something under the inspiration of the Lord? I don't think so!

65

When God is restoring or establishing truths, He purposely overemphasizes a biblical concept. God does this to say something to the Body of Christ at large. I truly believe that God is currently establishing a truth that is calling for a greater consciousness of the unreached people in our midst and what it takes to relate to them, while reaching them with our message. I praise God for every movement that is out there winning people to Christ. Like Paul said in Philippians 1:18 (NIV), "The important thing is that in every way...Christ is preached."

I have found that people who come in off the streets think, "Just help me get free from my addictions! Help me get to the place where my mind is right and I'm not tormented anymore!" The postmodern generation is asking, "Does it work?"

Paul said that prophecy and evangelism are supposed to go together. Notice what happens in this verse again (see 1 Cor. 14:24-25). When you prophesy it releases an atmosphere that goes to work on people's hearts simply by their just sitting in the midst of it. That's why we cannot eliminate the manifestations of the prophetic in an effort to make everyone comfortable. Paul tells us that if you have a prophetic anointing, it will begin to search your heart and begin to go to work on your soul. The Spirit of prophecy is an inclusive term describing the Holy Spirit energizing believers to speak inspired utterances to be shared publicly.

Oswald Chambers, the great writer, once said, "Spiritual truth is learned by atmosphere, not by intellectual reasoning." A prophetic spirit alters the atmosphere of our way of looking at things. If all are prophesying, that may not necessarily mean that you would have a specific word for every single person who passes through. But the Lord is searching and revealing people's hearts. The prophetic and evangelistic flows are working together to convince and to reveal.

What is the result when these two flows come together? Visitors and the unchurched are going to worship God, and they're going to report that God is among them. We want people to come and worship God, and truly know that "the presence of God is in this place"!

An evangelist is to be a prophet to the lost and emerging secular culture. The Greek word for prophesy is *propheteuo*, meaning "to speak under inspiration, to exercise the prophetic, to declare a thing which can only be known by divine revelation, to break forth under sudden impulse in praise of the divine counsels." A prophetic vessel speaks under inspiration of the Holy Spirit to comfort, edify, and encourage the Body. But the evangelist is the prophet to the lost culture. When I say "prophetic," I'm not referring to the office of a prophet, but to a gifting. I am referring to situational function. Prophetic ought to be more about the function rather than the title.

Fulfilling the Work of a Prophetic Evangelist

I charge you therefore before God and the Lord Jesus Christ, who will judge the living and the dead at His appearing and His kingdom: Preach the word! Be ready in season and out of season. Convince, rebuke, exhort, with all longsuffering and teaching. ...But you be watchful in all things, endure afflictions, do the work of an evangelist, fulfill your ministry (2 Timothy 4:1-2,5).

Characteristics of the Evangelist:

1. Evangelists enable churches to infiltrate their communities at the most relevant point. I believe that "new school evangelists" are going to be helping churches. They are not just going to be holding special meetings here and there; they are going to be working with local bodies doing regular outreaches to their communities.

2. Evangelists produce a breakthrough anointing with a transformational effect. There is an anointing that "breaks through" when dealing with lost society. It's an anointing that comes upon you to break through right to the heart.

3. Evangelists help with the understanding of how to integrate new believers into the Body of Christ. In my earlier days, I wrote a follow-up manual because I wanted to help maintain the souls who had come to Christ. Before I realized the term, I wanted to "conserve the fruit."

Characteristics of the Prophetic:

1. Prophets enable churches to navigate spiritual waters. A prophet's job is typically "in house" rather than "out of house." They

help with the understanding of God's purposes and with keeping a heavenly focus during turbulent times.

2. Prophets help with the identification of root issues and giftings that detonate something inside new converts. Prophets have insight that can bring focus and direction into a new convert's life. They are able, by God's grace, to bring clarity to God's implanted gift mixes, the gifting God has placed within believers.

3. Prophets reveal the hand of God in action and they make the enemy become visible.

In Order to Be a Prophetic Evangelist, You Must:

1. Be watchful. Make sure that your heart is right because you cannot share out of a bad heart and hope that someone else gets a good heart. You have to get your heart right because the message has to pass through you. You have to be watchful of the times and the patterns of people. God will show you things as you are watchful.

2. Endure afflictions. If you think about prophets in the Old Testament, and even prophets in the New Testament, they had extra warfare going on. When I'm doing what God wants me to do, I'm on the offensive and I'm throwing the blows. Sometimes, however, we're preoccupied with blocking the enemy's punches when really some of us need to get on the offense and begin to win some people to the Lord.

3. Do the work of an evangelist. The evangelist is on the front line of God's army. They have a burning desire to reach the unreached in this world. Everywhere they go they're preaching the gospel, and signs and wonders are following. Being on the front line means that one of the things that God gives an evangelist is boldness. What if these things could come together? Why not? They are distinct offices, but I believe the two anointings can rest upon all believers. The Bible says that your sons and daughters shall prophesy (see Joel 2:28). The Bible says we are to fulfill the work of an evangelist. So if we're to prophesy and we're to fulfill the work of an evangelist, we can also be prophetic evangelists!

WHEN SILAS MET PAUL

It seemed good to us, being assembled with one accord, to send chosen men to you with our beloved Barnabas and Paul (Acts 15:25).

We know Barnabas and Paul were apostles. People back in Jerusalem were a little fearful of Saul of Tarsus because he had been involved in persecuting Christians in the early Church. But Saul (Paul) had a genuine conversion. Barnabas was the one who extended a line of credibility and said that he believed in Paul.

Now Barnabas was determined to take with them John called Mark. But Paul insisted that they should not take with them the one who had departed from them in Pamphylia, and had not gone with them to the work (Acts 15:37-38).

Barnabas and Paul decided to go different ways due to a disagreement on whether or not John Mark should come with them. John Mark had abandoned them after one particular episode when they had a major power encounter. Paul's issue was that he didn't want to take this kid with them anymore. He was concerned that John Mark would bail on them again.

Now, here's my question. Why did Paul choose Silas? He could have chosen Andrew; he could have also chosen Thomas. There were other apostles. Why Silas, and why at this time? Paul knew that he was appointed as an apostle, and that God had called him to do mission work. Apostolic work primarily involves evangelism, and seeing the gospel lived out in its recipients.

Paul was being led of the Lord very strategically. He knew that he would benefit from linking himself with the gifting in another. Barnabas and Paul were both apostles, and both similarly gifted. But Paul chose Silas. I truly believe that Paul saw the benefit of having the prophetic anointing embodied in Silas.

What is the next thing that happened? Paul and Silas went around strengthening the churches. Paul the Apostle was involved on the front lines, doing cutting-edge missions work, but he was predominately

69

evangelistic. Considering what he would run into, he would need the prophetic to meet the evangelistic.

Prophets have a strong sense of mission and they live with a strong sense of identity. They are used to rejection; it's part of the prophetic makeup; they get rejected. I think Paul knew what he was getting in Silas. He needed a guy who would stick with it.

Here are some similarities between the two anointings of the prophetic and evangelism:

1. Often both anointings begin with receiving a burden. When I begin to prophesy and I look at someone, one of the first things that rise up within me is a burden for them. When I know I'm being led to witness to someone, I will feel a deep compassion for them.

2. Both anointings act as catalysts. The prophet is the visionary, and the evangelist wants to get more people saved and keep the church moving. You don't get stuck in a rut when you're in a church where both of these anointings are present. Your church will be pioneering; it will be advancing. Your church will be trailblazing; it will be on the cutting edge!

3. Both anointings are resilient as they encounter unusual warfare and rejection. The key here is to understand that there will be a need for greater "toughness" in dealing with darkness. God graces these giftings with "flint for foreheads" (see Ezek. 3:9), which is an ability to be invincible to hell's backlash.

4. Both anointings are mouthpieces for God. They are both strategic to the end-time scenario. We have heard of prophetic intercession, and I believe this is right on. I believe that we are going to hear more about prophetic evangelism. It is definitely on the radar.

PROPHETIC EVANGELISTIC ACTS

I know individuals who have done prophetic acts. These acts seem to release liberty and freedom in an individual while they affect others for deliverance. I also believe that everyone can participate in prophetic evangelistic acts.

Let me give you three categories of the prophetic acts I'm referring to:

1. Spontaneous light and trumpet acts.

And so it was, when Gideon heard the telling of the dream and its interpretation, that he worshiped. He returned to the camp of Israel, and said, "Arise, for the Lord has delivered the camp of Midian into your hand." Then he divided the three hundred men into three companies, and he put a trumpet into every man's hand, with empty pitchers, and torches inside the pitchers. And he said to them, "Look at me and do likewise; watch, and when I come to the edge of the camp you shall do as I do: When I blow the trumpet, I and all who are with me, then you also blow the trumpets on every side of the whole camp, and say, 'The sword of the Lord and of Gideon!'" So Gideon and the hundred men who were with him came to the outpost of the camp at the beginning of the middle watch, just as they had posted the watch; and they blew the trumpets and broke the pitchers that were in their hands. Then the three companies blew the trumpets and broke the pitchers—they held the torches in their left hands and the trumpets in their right hands for blowing—and they cried, "The sword of the Lord and of Gideon!" And every man stood in his place all around the camp; and the whole army ran and cried out and fled (Judges 7:15-21).

Where did Gideon get that idea? Do you think he sat around with a few guys one day and said, "I know how we can defeat this army! We'll go out with some trumpets, we'll each have a pitcher with a big lighter in it, and we're going to mess those guys up. We're going to blow a trumpet in their ears and throw a pitcher with a big lighter on them and they are going to be like, AAAHHH! They're going to run out so fast they won't know what hit them!" No, this had to be a prophetic evangelistic act—a spontaneous light and trumpet act.

The Scriptures don't give the impression that there was even any combat going on. They did all of this and the enemy miraculously fled. A spontaneous light and trumpet act is when God gives you a strategy and it involves a spontaneous witness where you proclaim and radiate light.

You didn't go with the intention to witness; it was spontaneous when you broke your pitcher and your light had to shine. You didn't even prepare beforehand what you were going to speak, but in a moment, you knew you had to stand up and say something. All of a sudden when you do that act, someone gets saved.

I've had instances where I didn't go to a place thinking I was going to witness to anyone. I didn't prepare in my heart to say, "Okay, this is what I'm going to preach." I just simply walked into a situation and recognized that I needed to let my light shine. It's like the torch inside the pitcher, but God has me break out, and light shines, and I'm immediately given a trumpet.

To blow a trumpet is a very prophetic thing; it's to proclaim the word of the Lord. A trumpet blows a distinct signal. I think you're going to find yourself in these types of situations. When you think back, you will know that it was one of those prophetic evangelistic acts God was asking you to do.

Notice this, Gideon had to go to the enemies' camp. He couldn't just do this in his own camp and blow the trumpets, throw the pitchers, and then somehow the enemies' camp is defeated. Why is it we don't want to go where the lost people are? It's like wanting to fish but not going out to a pond where the fish live. Are you going to fish in your bathtub or in your kitchen sink where it's comfortable? If you want to catch fish, you have to go where the fish live.

2. Dying-to-self and abandonment acts.

Most assuredly, I say to you, unless a grain of wheat falls into the ground and dies, it remains alone; but if it dies, it produces much grain (John 12:24).

I believe that there will be divine prophetic evangelistic acts that will also fall into this dying-to-self and abandonment category. These acts are instructions from the Lord that call for sacrifice and unusual abandonment. Typically, you're acting in the opposite spirit of what is represented in the predominate culture.

This act often includes maintaining a stance in the midst of persecution. Jesus said that you will be persecuted, but He will give you the words to say and this will stand as a testimony (see Mark 13:9-11).

One day my nephew, Frankie, was in his junior high class. When the teacher was done with the lesson, there were still five minutes left in the class. The teacher turned and said to them, "Okay students, here's what we're going to do. We're going to practice this Buddha technique for the next five minutes." He then proceeds to lead the whole class in a Buddha technique.

Frankie had started a Bible club, the very first in the history of that junior high school. When the teacher had finished, with only one minute left in the class, he asked, "Does anyone have any final questions?" My nephew lifted his hand and said, "No sir, but can I make a statement? You just showed us how Buddhism could help us in five minutes; can I show you how Jesus Christ can change your life in one split second? All you have to do is call upon the name of Jesus."

Here was this kid, his voice was cracking, but he stood in front of everyone in that class and told them about Jesus. Two girls went to his Bible club and got saved. That was a prophetic evangelistic act. More than just words come off of your lips when a dying-to-self act is released. We're always thinking about what we should say and how we should say it, but prophetic evangelism is more about obedience than the elegance of your words.

3. Stretching-yourself-out-on-them identification acts.

And he went up and lay on the child, and put his mouth on his mouth, his eyes on his eyes, and his hands on his hands; and he stretched himself out on the child, and the flesh of the child became warm (2 Kings 4:34).

In other words, I've got to see what they're seeing; I've got to speak what they're hearing (their language); I need to feel what they're feeling. I believe that these acts are following a holy summons from the Lord to serve and identify with the lost in a way that we are being stretched beyond our comfort zones. Elisha had to stretch out on the boy.

My wife has to take a class on First Aid because she's becoming certified to perform CPR. There are times, if someone is dying and their life is on the line, that you stretch out on them. It is a prophetic evangelistic act of sacrifice when you stretch yourself out beyond a comfort zone. It also causes the hearer to warm up to what we are saying due to our connection with them.

RESULTS OF PROPHETIC EVANGELISM

Revelation and insight. The reason that I want to have the prophetic and the evangelistic anointing is because if I'm witnessing to someone, I want God to reveal that person's heart. I want insight into that heart. When both of these anointings are operating within me, I believe I will be able to more effectively witness.

Fresh inspiration. I think sometimes we get stale in our witness, stale in our approach. Sometimes we get stuck and we just "don't feel like it." The prophetic releases things that will allow us to be inspired. We don't want to witness to anyone when we're down, but the prophetic anointing will release fresh inspiration.

Weaponry and strategic tools versus the darkness. Prophetic evangelism is a weapon against darkness; that's why the enemy hates the prophetic so much. Prophetic evangelism flies under radar, so that darkness has trouble negating the effect. With this "spiritual combo" tool, it becomes a strategic key to unlocking the tough situations.

Enthusiasm and life. The Greek word for enthusiasm is *entheos*, which means "God in you; God breathed." When you're out witnessing, there's something on you, something about you. I got saved because I heard something that a guy was talking about, but I also looked at him, and I wanted what he had to also be on me. There was something on him that witnessed to me.

Creative powers and change. The spoken word is creative and it brings about change. When things come into formation in someone's life, you're able to turn a new page in the heavenlies.

The best way I can communicate this concept to you is to relate an analogy. Years ago, in the weight loss industry, there were two different camps. One group of expert nutritionists told us to watch what we eat (reduce calories) in order to reach our weight goals. Another group of experts were into exercise and they told us to train harder to burn more calories. In the latest wave of technology in weight loss, everyone agrees that diet combined with exercise achieves the most effective results. In the same way, my prayer is that our two camps of evangelism and the prophetic would combine for God's glory.

ACTION STEP ADDENDUM

When Prophecy Met Evangelism in Our Church: The Testimony of the International Church of Las Vegas

(This section is written by Pastor Paul Goulet, Senior Pastor of the International Church of Las Vegas—www.ICLV.com.)

When we moved to Las Vegas, Nevada, we were not prepared for what we would encounter. Although we wanted revival in Las Vegas, we did not know how to make it happen.

I found out very quickly that all of my counseling tools and techniques could not bring revival to Las Vegas. I had a Master's degree, I had graduated with highest honors from a seminary, and I had started a counseling center. I was very successful, but then God called me to be a pastor in Las Vegas. When we got to Las Vegas, there was a higher call on my life, and I knew that what was in me was not enough to change my city.

In 1994, I was touched by the power of God through fasting and prayer and I really didn't know what to do with it. Soon after, a friend treated us to a pastor's conference in Canada. My wife and I walked in and saw people getting blasted by the Holy Spirit. I looked at my wife and said, "Honey, what do you think?" She turned to me and said, "This reminds me of an asylum." I echoed her thoughts and concluded that they all needed therapy.

But then came the last night. I went up to one of the prayer team workers and I asked, "Will you pray for revival in Las Vegas?" The guy said, "No, I want to pray for you." So I smiled politely and said, "Go ahead." He prayed for me, and I actually fell down.

While I was down on the floor I prayed one of the most dangerous prayers I've ever prayed. I said, "God, while I'm down here why don't You go ahead and do whatever You want to me." I'm on the ground and all of a sudden my body starts shaking. It was so embarrassing! Then people started gathering around me prophesying, "Souls, thousands of souls!" The more they prophesied the more I shook uncontrollably.

We came back to Vegas; I was hoping that nothing weird would happen again. Before that time we didn't really have the power of God, so if you don't have the power, you at least have good programs, right?

In the first six months of our pastorate we had started directing our church to become more seeker sensitive.

All this changed our first Sunday back. I started shaking uncontrollably as we started the worship. All I could think about was how badly I needed to get myself under control. But the more I fought it, the more the power of God came on me. Finally, I stumbled up to the platform, held on to the pulpit, and said, "If you want the power of God, come up here!" I couldn't believe what I had just said. To my surprise almost everyone came forward.

I didn't know what to do next. We were Assemblies of God and I know that we're supposed to receive the baptism and speak in tongues, but I had never experienced anything like this before. I had always believed in the power, but had felt like I had no "gun powder" in my bullets. I would pray for people and they would get sicker; I would pray for people for the baptism and nothing would happen. Everything changed that day in our church.

As the crowd filled the altar, I stood paralyzed with surprise. What should I do next? Looking back on that day rekindles strong emotions of gratitude to God. His power shook our congregation in ways that are difficult to describe. Men, women, and children fell under that power without ever a touch. Bodies were healed. Some even had visions. We had been swept away by a mighty wave. By the time the second service was supposed to start, bodies were still on the ground. I was hoping to regain control of myself and my reputation, but instead the Holy Spirit gave me words of knowledge, faith, and boldness.

Many experienced the power of God and prophetic gifts for the first time. But within one week, 100 members left the church. I was devastated. I thought the church members wanted the power of God. I didn't know where to turn or what to do.

I'll never forget how I grieved the Holy Spirit just a few months after this great day. I told the Holy Spirit, "Don't touch me like that anymore. It embarrassed me." Pride got in the way; I kept worrying about people's opinions of me. Here the Holy Spirit was pouring out the power, the prophetic, signs and wonders, but I cared more about people's approval. The Holy Spirit was rocking our world, but we chose to get off the ride. Isn't it incredible that the Holy Spirit is a gentleman? He didn't force Himself on me; instead He withdrew. We lost a hundred people in one week, but after I grieved the Holy Spirit our church started to grow again. We went back to the normal services. No miracles, no signs and wonders, but people started coming. We had church growth, we had land, we had a building; people said we were heroes again, but in my heart I knew that I had grieved the Holy Spirit. For one and a half years I prayed for another chance, and I learned that God is the God of another chance.

My second chance came at a conference where Steve Hill and Claudio Freidzon were speaking. During the second session, Claudio delivered a word of knowledge, "Someone here has been praying for a second chance. Come up here right now." I did not hesitate one moment; I ran to the front. I didn't care what anyone thought anymore. All I wanted was one more chance for the power of God to flow through my life and see lives changed forever.

I ran up there, and Claudio waved his hand and said, "Receive it; take it." The power of God hit me. I fell to the ground and heard the Lord speak to me clearly. "Paul, do you really want the power of God?" I said, "Yes, Lord." He then said, "This time you have to die." I saw a vision of my hand on the sinner's cross and I saw the spike going through my hand. I saw the blood start pouring out, and He said, "Paul, are you willing to give up your pride and your people-pleasing?" I said, "Yes, Lord."

By the time I got off the ground, I was a transformed person. I knew exactly what I had to do. I needed to confess to my church about grieving the Holy Spirit. I also had to see if this incredible power would flow through me like it did through Claudio.

The first Sunday back was my opportunity to make things right. First step was confession, second step was teaching them the Word, and third step was impartation.

I stood there and said, "As your pastor, I confess that I grieved the Holy Spirit. I cared more about the approval of people than the approval of God. With God's help I will never do that again; please forgive me. I've already asked for God's forgiveness, but I ask you as the church to forgive me. From now on all of these services are God's services and not mine. If you want this power, come back tonight at 6:00."

To my surprise the evening service was packed. I explained what impartation was all about and then I said, "If you want the power of God, come up here." They started lining up and the power of God moved; hundreds were filled with the Holy Spirit.

Some were delivered; others were healed.

Since 1996 our leaders have been equipped and filled by the Holy Spirit. The gifts of the Spirit flow freely in our services and in our community. A city like Las Vegas can only be transformed by transformed believers. Each time the power of God moves in our services, I remind the people that He is touching us to use us to win souls, change homes, cities, and the world. I am not very concerned or impressed when people cry, fall, shake, or laugh. I am very concerned with what happens to them after they stand up. Will they become a disciple, a witness, a world-changer?

Our church has never been the same since we invited the prophetic into our services. Every Sunday several thousand attend services. The Lord has given us a vision to plant 2,000 churches by the year 2020. He has also given us a strategy to reach this vision. Since 1996 we have helped start "on fire" ministry training centers in India, Mexico, Egypt, and Las Vegas. Many churches have already been started by our graduates.

It is clear to all of us at ICLV that God is more than willing to use people like you and me. He wants to touch you with His power, but He also wants to transform you. Our world is crying out for the supernatural. They are more open to God's power than ever before. Ask God to fill you with His Spirit today. Then ask Him to use you to change the world. I can assure you that the gifts of prophecy and others will facilitate and empower your soul-winning ventures.

The apostle Paul's words sum up this concept the best:

And my speech and my preaching were not with persuasive words of human wisdom, but in demonstration of the Spirit and of power, that your faith should not be in the wisdom of men but in the power of God (1 Corinthians 2:4-5).

May we be able to say the same thing in years to come.

CHAPTER 4

FAITH FOR AN END-TIME AWAKENING

MANY TIMES I HAVE HAD DREAMS of seeing stadiums full of people coming to hear the gospel and getting saved by the multiple thousands. In fact, I was called to full-time ministry after a full week of having these God-inspired dreams. These special glimpses have left me undone to see and experience what the Holy Spirit has downloaded into my heart.

There is an end-time harvest coming, the magnitude of which will stagger the average Christian's thinking. There is a biblical term *kairos*, which is used to portray a seasonable time that is fraught with once-in-a-lifetime opportunities. Jesus used this word in Matthew 13:30, describing a "time of harvest" that would be on a whole new scale.

You may be experiencing an urging or intense desire that God is stirring within you—something you know that you need to step into immediately. Each time we respond to His urging in obedience, we see another installment in the fulfillment of God's purposes. This is referred to as prophetic fulfillment.

Having a fresh sense of prophetic fulfillment provokes prophetic evangelists to greater levels of effectiveness. This is an important understanding to have in times of darkness. In fact, the destiny of the multitudes seem to rest on you and I realizing this!

DIVINE DRAMA

We're living in dark times and there could be the sense that our impact in the Church is going to be minimal. We live in a dramatic world where people face great hindrances with excessive drama. Their dreams have died, their hopes have died, and their opportunities have died. There's a spirit of futility that says no matter what I do, no matter how long I do it, it doesn't matter, because things are not going to change, so why even try? This spirit causes a laid-back, futon-faith Christianity. It's easy today to feel like nothing good is left to happen.

When you are down to nothing, God is up to something! God has drama for you also—divine drama. God has an amazing track record, and His résumé for doing special things during dark seasons is flawless.

INSIDER INFORMATION

And Jesus cried out again with a loud voice, and yielded up His spirit. Then, behold, the veil of the temple was torn in two from top to bottom; and the earth quaked, and the rocks were split, and the graves were opened; and many bodies of the saints who had fallen asleep were raised; and coming out of the graves after His resurrection, they went into the holy city and appeared to many. So when the centurion and those with him, who were guarding Jesus, saw the earthquake and the things that had happened, they feared greatly, saying, "Truly this was the Son of God!" (Matthew 27:50-54)

Matthew 27 is about the backstage pass. We get to see what happened behind the scenes when we read this account. In today's world, we need to see behind the scenes, because if all we see in the world is what the evening news tells us, we're going to be discouraged. We're not going to think that we can make any kind of difference.

God wants you to know you are His very intention! He has destined you for this very moment! This is a mighty time to be alive, even in the midst of chaos.

A TOUGH SELL

Faith for an end-time mass harvest begins with the Word of God, yet includes testimonies (the working out of God's Word). God often boosts a renewed confidence in His promises by turning a tough, improbable case into a highlight of His glory. Outside of Apostle Paul, the Roman guard at the foot of the cross may qualify for the most improbable conversion in ancient history.

What was it that would cause a hardened centurion who had seen one crucifixion after another, raised on the Roman polytheistic belief of many gods, reared on violence, loyal to Rome, to come to the end of his working day and say, "Truly this was the Son of God"? What was it that in the midst of this darkness could birth such light? What is it that God specializes in when all hope is gone? This centurion's turnaround gives me hope for this generation. If this centurion would arrive at this confession in the midst of an unpromising situation, we can believe for our own tough cases. This man mirrors the generation at hand.

The centurion was not predisposed for any spiritual event. He didn't recognize that what was happening was of the one true God. At 12:00 noon, for no explained reason, there was a three-hour total solar eclipse. Then he heard this Man, Jesus, cry out, "Eli, Eli, lama sabachthani" and all of a sudden the darkness vanished and it was daylight again.

God is speaking into your spirit right now with this story from history; God is going to interrupt the darkness! He's going to resurrect His Church and clothe it in resplendent glory to break the darkness. We are in that three hours of darkness right now in our world today. The reason why darkness fell over the land was because the light was obscured. Do we let our light get obscured? Could the real issue be that our light is not shining?

Some of the people we never thought would get saved will get saved. Isaiah 9:2-3 tells us that "the people who walked in darkness have seen a great light." We're entering into that "great light" moment in history. Isaiah goes on to say, "They rejoice before You according to the joy of harvest." This period in history will be characterized by the harvest joy flowing from the prophetic evangelist across the globe.

A CURTAIN CALL

Let's look at the most revered holy curtain in history. It was in the temple, and once a year, one man got a chance to have a backstage pass. He had bells attached to him to let folks know he was still moving because if there were sins in his life and the bells weren't ringing, his "bells had been rung," if you know what I mean, and they would have to pull his dead body out. "Next!" The priests had to be right before God.

What was behind that curtain? There was a box where God's presence dwelled, but today He lives in you! God ripped that curtain from top to bottom and what was behind that curtain was Heaven on earth. He said, "I'm going to rip the veil of confusion, not just because I want to let you in, but because I want to get out and let Heaven touch your world." God wants to rip apart the veil of confusion in your world, your identity, and your image. When people don't know the Lord, they have a veil before their eyes and can't see clearly. The truth is there all the time, but people can't see it when they're looking through a veil. It's like trying to see a beautiful tree out your window, but when you look through sheer curtains, you only see a blurry image. It's not until you pull the curtain away that you can see clearly.

A WHOLE LOT OF SHAKING GOING ON

Back to the scene at the cross. The curtain split from top to bottom and all of a sudden an earthquake shook the area! Now California is somewhat used to some shaking, but the Bible says that rocks split open. I believe we are going to experience a move of God that will be equivalent to a "moral" earthquake; it will seize hearts and affect lives.

Right before our eyes, God is going to break long-standing obstacles! When you think you just can't get past this person or this situation, God is going to break the rocks right in front of you. He is going to plant His cause in the epicenter of your heart and it will fuel new exploits in your life. When you align yourself with the cause of God, rocks have got to move out of the way! We must be consumed with the cause of God.

Just as in that time, when many bodies came up out of their graves, God wants to resurrect things that have died in you. You may think that your window of opportunity is past the time that anything good can happen, but remember we serve the God of the resurrection.

Just like God brought signs that convinced the Roman guard, He is at work behind the scenes to pull hearts in the direction of their destiny. Tear up your "un-savable" list of people who seem too lost to ever get saved.

BUSINESS AS USUAL—NOT!

Signs from Heaven furnish us with prophetic fuel so that we can have courage and spiritual energy to rise up and reap the harvest regardless of the world's condition. It's so important to know what time it is. God's reign—His kingdom—is not ruled by calendars and clocks, but by seasons. We're in a unique season today. I've never seen so many church leaders entering into 40-day fasts. I've never seen so many people giving themselves to 24-hour prayer meetings, healing rooms, and concerts of prayer.

You don't sow like that without having a monumental reaping. It's time to harvest; it's time to pray; it's time to fast; it's time to get out there. He's moving us into a new season.

> *Besides this you know what [a critical] hour this is, how it is high time now for you to wake up out of your sleep (rouse to reality). For salvation (final deliverance) is nearer to us now than when we first believed (adhered to, trusted in, and relied on Christ, the Messiah)* (Romans 13:11 AMP).

This verse predicates our action and activity in this new season upon knowing what time it is. People are ripe and hungry right now. People are so desperate that they're trying to tap into the spiritual realm because they want encouragement and meaning. Those of us who know the gospel have a clarion call that we have got something to give to this world. This is a critical hour. This hour has more to do with the activities in the heavenlies than the activities of earth.

This new season is the hour of the Spirit. The challenge in this hour is not just seeing the natural situations in what the evening news can tell you, but by what the Spirit of God is declaring. There's a new page turning in the heavenlies and it's time for us to wake up!

You and I have been brought to the stage of history for such a time as this. It's not an accident that you and I were born at this time. We're going to witness miracles that no generation has witnessed yet.

TWO SCHOOLS OF THOUGHT

When you talk to people about the current move of God, there are two schools of thought. There are some who would say we're in judgment:

"Our country is under judgment and it's all over, baby!" They say God is now releasing the bowls of wrath; that we're in the midst of judgment. Many feel judgment is being executed because we're beyond repair, evidenced by the fact that we can't seem to stop the modern rupturing of sanity and morality.

But the second school of thought is that righteousness needs to be executed. Yes, there's darkness, but as long as God's anointing is on His people, His influence is still moving and it's not too late. God is still patient and willing for folks to repent.

The first school of thought is that we're beyond repair. The second school of thought is that we're beyond excuse.

Thus says the Lord: "Execute judgment and righteousness, and deliver the plundered out of the hand of the oppressor. Do no wrong and do no violence to the stranger, the fatherless, or the widow, nor shed innocent blood in this place" (Jeremiah 22:3).

This is a "now" Scripture. God is saying that both schools of thought are playing out. Judgment and righteousness need to be executed simultaneously. You don't have to think it's one or the other.

No matter what camp you're in, you're not excused. It is time to deliver the plunder out of the hand of the oppressor. As Charles Finney, a 19th-century revivalist, said, "Do not tell me of the rising floods of evil, but let me tell you of the rising floods of grace." The grace of God always releases deliverance to captured hearts.

We must have faith to be used in mass evangelism. During this age, our job is to be more focused than ever before on how to see our friends, family, and neighbors come to Christ. We must focus on the potential divine appointments that God would lead us into to be able to deliver people out of the hand of the oppressor.

TWO SICKLES, TWO OUTCOMES

Faith for an end-time awakening comes from perceiving and believing the promises of God that relate to the times. The Book of Revelation divulges that two sickles are thrust into the earth. One sickle is for judgment and the other for reaping massive worldwide harvest. The apostle John received the insight into the eternal strategy of God in Revelation 14:15 where it says, "Thrust in Your sickle and reap, for the time has come for You to reap, for the harvest of the earth is ripe."

This sickle of global harvest precedes the sickle of global judgment. This is consistent with God's desire to go with mercy before judgment. Understanding these concepts has always been used of God to call forth an inner compulsion in His children to thrust themselves in the harvest. God is calling His Church to a new Christian activism. In light of this revelation, to carry on in a watered-down state of limited activity in evangelism demonstrates that unbelief has replaced faith in one's heart.

DISASTER PREVENTION

One day, Jesus wept over the inhabitants of Jerusalem due to their inability to detect their opportunity. In Luke 19:41-44, Jesus' eyes moistened with tears because their eyes were blinded to their time of visitation. Jerusalem was to have a sickle of harvest, but instead they would experience the sickle of judgment.

Their eventual landscape, their resulting predicament, would ultimately reflect their ignorance and negligence. Our landscapes may well be a reflection of some of our modern oversights and lack of recognition coupled with inactivity.

Jesus declares in Matthew 5:13 that we are the salt of the earth. Salt possesses the power to give flavor and stop corruption, to fertilize. It makes its absence or presence felt, and exerts a distinct effect as it is dispersed. Salt is a catch-all symbol that refers to doing whatever it takes to preserve God's deposit and restrain the spoiling agent in our world today. If Jesus says, "You are the salt of the earth," He's also ordaining your impact in your world simply by decreeing this fact.

DYING ON THE VINE

"But if you will not hear these words, I swear by Myself," says the Lord, "that this house shall become a desolation" (Jeremiah 22:5).

Statistics have said that in the next five years, one out of every six Protestant churches will close their doors. You might think, "Those poor Protestant people." Time out—we are those Protestant people! Churches that are not giving themselves to soul winning are churches that are dying on the vine. We must hear God's cry to fulfill the Great Commission.

I've never come across a Christian who was a passionate soul winner who was backsliding. I suppose it's possible, but people who are consistent in winning people to Christ relive their own salvation!

I pray that you may be active in sharing your faith, so that you will have a full understanding of every good thing we have in Christ (Philemon 1:6 NIV).

When you are actively winning souls, you become appreciative of your own salvation. In the process of presenting the gift of Jesus with someone, you're opening to yourself a more full understanding of what you already have.

The Bible lets us know that people who win souls reap rewards. Churches that have this evangelistic spirit about them are places where missionaries are raised up and folks are sent out. Any effort by a church or an individual to put their hands to the plow to win souls will see that God causes their finances to continue to come in. The opposite is also true. If you don't hear the words, your house becomes desolated.

One of the greatest threats of the generation that we live in is that we may become like our environment. Any individual or church that doesn't wake up and witness will soon become a shared commodity of what surrounds it.

The Bible says there's great joy over just one sinner who converts. Evangelist Charles Finney believed that whenever he felt the grace of

God slow down upon his works, he needed to go out and win someone to the Lord. This always changes the one doing the witnessing, as well as the one being witnessed to. Christians who are not actively sharing the joy of their salvation are losing the joy of their salvation.

> *"To be a soul winner is the happiest thing in the world.*
> *With every soul you bring to Christ, you*
> *get a new Heaven upon earth."*
> —C.H. Spurgeon

Take Action

In Luke chapter 6, Jesus tells the man with the withered arm to stretch it out. This guy's arm was atrophied and just hanging down at his side. The right arm of the Church—outreach—is withered. This man had a withered arm because of lack of use. It's very interesting that Jesus told him to stretch it out. He didn't walk over and pull on his arm, but He spoke a command for the man to stretch out his arm. The man could have said, "I'd like to, Jesus, but I've got some problems here. You see, my arm is withered and has no strength, so I can't do that." But the moment he moved his arm in obedience to reach out, it became fully functioning!

The miracle that happened to the man with the withered arm didn't happen until he stretched out his arm! It is the same with us. We won't see our miracle until we stretch out our arm—the arm of outreach.

Rolling Like a River

God is saying that we need to break out of spiritual ruts. We need to begin to allow a stream of living water to flow out of us. We need to engage lost humanity. Something miraculous starts to happen when we break out of spiritual isolation.

Let's look at Ezekiel; he has a vision of the temple and a stream of water that gradually becomes wider and more powerful. Look what happens when the river goes into the sea.

> *And it shall be that every living thing that moves, wherever the rivers go, will live. There will be a very great multitude of fish, because these waters go there; for they will be healed, and everything will live wherever the river goes* (Ezekiel 47:9).

This passage promises healing and a "very great multitude of fish" because the river flows. There is going to be something God will start in His Church that will end up out on the streets of major cities that will release massive harvests.

Isn't it interesting that the Holy Spirit says the waters have to go there? Without the water going there, there won't be a great multitude of fish. The waters, which represent what God has deposited within us, must reach the sea, which represents the masses of humanity who are without Christ.

STOPPED UP WITH SELF-CENTEREDNESS

The Dead Sea is stagnant because nothing flows out of it. It's like the Christian who gets a lot of great teaching at church, goes to outside conferences, receives tons of prayer, but nothing God puts in ever flows out. It is a bad case of self-centeredness winning out over self-denial.

A true apostolic movement is when every aspect of the Body of Christ is doing their job to win the lost to Jesus Christ. There's no way around it. The waters can't be stopped. The Lord wants us to spring a leak! God has put something inside of us and He wants it to flow out. The more it flows out, the more life it's going to bring. If there's only a trickle at first, He wants it to become a mighty river. It affects lives; it brings healing! It brings deliverance!

There ought to be life coming out of you wherever you go—your neighborhood, your workplace, your schoolyard. Wherever there's a dry place—a need—the waters need to go there.

BEWARE: SWAMPS AND MARSHES AHEAD

But here's the sober warning: swamps and marshes ahead. Swamps represent what happens when (1) Church bodies turn inward and cease to have a purpose beyond themselves, and (2) Individuals stay in perpetual recovery.

But its swamps and marshes will not be healed; they will be given over to salt (Ezekiel 47:11).

Here's the deal, swamps and marshes are places where water gets stuck. When water doesn't flow anywhere, it eventually turns to salt.

God says to us that because you don't go there, because you won't flow there, you're going to be given over to salt.

We're either going to be given as salt to the world, as it says in Matthew 5:13, where we are a preservative and seasoning, a good thing; or we'll be given over to become as dead-end salt before the world, a bad thing. Nothing can live in that kind of salt. It's a curse, a judgment. Either way, we will have a salt encounter.

Harvest Theology

Let me go deep for a moment to build your faith for a harvest of souls. Three times a year the nation of Israel was to gather to the Lord in Jerusalem to celebrate festival occasions. These three yearly feasts were referred to as the Feast of Passover, the Feast of Pentecost, and the Feast of Tabernacles. The feasts are prophetic types, foreshadowing the future events that Christ fulfilled in His body. Interestingly, they also set forth a blueprint of the ministry of Jesus relative to the plan of redemption. The Feast of Pentecost, also known as the Feast of Harvest, was the second of the three great annual festivals. It's called the Feast of Harvest because it concluded the harvest of the latter grains and the day of the first fruits (see Exod. 23:16). The second feast came at the time of the corn and wheat harvest, the first harvest, which came as a result of the spring rains. This harvest pointed to the fruit harvest, which came at the end of the year. In the same way that this festival pointed to a future harvest of grain and signaled the outpouring of the Spirit, it also served as a promise that Christ came to fulfill.

This spiritual picture was seen in a physical type on the day of Pentecost in the Book of Acts, when God unleashed 3,000 souls at Pentecost and another 5,000 soon thereafter (see Acts 4:4). God was communicating that these 8,000 souls were the first fruits of a later massive harvest. This redemptive release prophesies of a latter rain harvest of immense proportions before Jesus' return. God was giving the Church a down payment harvest, which was a physical type of a spiritual feast that He set in motion millenniums beforehand.

The bottom line is that we, as the last-day Church, had better get ready. Just imagine what magnitude of the harvest would be needed to fulfill the end-time ultimate installment of souls God has promised us through His Feasts!

MADE FOR STADIUMS

There will be a great multitude of fish; literally thousands will be saved in ordinary church services. I believe the huge stadiums that are being built for sporting events will end up really being used for Christian services. I challenge you to live your life believing there will be a great harvest coming.

In Genesis 8:22, God made this promise, "While the earth remains, seedtime and harvest...shall not cease." This was part of a covenant God gave to Noah and the generations to follow. The fluctuating times of seedtime and harvest are divine things, not human things. The kingdom of God operates under certain governing laws and this is ordained to give the believer the opportunity to sow new seed and expect greater harvest. The changing of seasons is God's sovereignty to cause the earth to be fruitful and bring forth a harvest. There will always be harvest time in every generation.

EXTREME MYTH MAKEOVERS

I would like to debunk some commonly believed church myths:

Myth #1—The day of mass conversions is over.

No, my Bible says there will be a very great multitude of fish to come because the waters will go there. Jesus said in Matthew 4:19 that He will make you "fishers of men." The word "make" in that verse means to declare, to speak prophetically. God is prophetically speaking over His Church, declaring there is going to be a very great harvest. The seeds of the harvest planted by the massive prayer movement will bear great fruit in this season. We should press forward for no less than one billion souls worldwide in this decade.

Amos, the prophet, declared in Amos 9:13 that "the days are coming...when the plowman shall overtake the reaper." This speaks of a mass harvest that spills into every season, a harvest no longer limited to a predictable quantity.

Myth #2—Moves of God will only happen in certain geographical locations.

People in America tend to think all of the needs are in faraway places. It's easy to think, "China, yes; Africa, yes; but the U.S.A.?"

The Bible says in Habakkuk 2:14, "As the waters cover the sea, the earth will be filled with the knowledge of His glory." Notice this; it didn't just say the knowledge of God. It's the glory of the Lord! It's tangible; it's weighty. This glory and its knowledge will be convincing and overwhelming upon the hearts of the inhabitants of the earth.

He's saying in this verse that the waters cover the earth—not just China, not just Africa, not just South America. But let me tell you, it will be inner city Los Angeles, San Francisco, Las Vegas, New York—wherever there is a place for water to go, God says His glory is going to come!

Myth #3—It's too evil today for anything to change.

Arise, shine; For your light has come! And the glory of the Lord is risen upon you. For behold, the darkness shall cover the earth, and deep darkness the people; but the Lord will arise over you, And His glory will be seen upon you. The Gentiles shall come to your light, and kings to the brightness of your rising (Isaiah 60:1-3).

Don't let it surprise you—the Lord will arise over you! The unbelievers will come to the light. The abundance of the sea will be turned over to you. The sea means all of humanity. God is saying He wants to give you a nation. I believe that there are going to be whole nations where righteousness will prevail. That doesn't mean that every single person in the country will be a believer, but the leadership and dominant spirit will belong to the Lord.

I will give you the treasures of darkness And hidden riches of secret places, that you may know that I, the Lord... (Isaiah 45:3).

Look at that—treasures out of darkness! You may have a son or a daughter who is so far gone. You may have a boss who is cold and hard; how about all of the famous people who society thinks could never get saved? God is going to give you treasures—people who will be trophies in the kingdom! The harvest is a treasure to God. The water has just got to go there, and then God will get some treasures out of darkness.

Myth #4—The Church has already seen its greatest hour.

God's timetable for history's conclusion is connected with the Great Commission!

You think the Book of Acts had some mighty things in it? Well, we ain't seen nothin' yet! We serve a God who saves the best wine for last. The latter glory will be greater than the former glory.

Don't despair or get heart sick over past outreach attempts that have fallen short of your expectations. Get ready for a net-breaking catch of a lifetime!

In James 5:7-8, the end-time scenario is likened to a farmer who waits for a latter rain which produces a bumper crop of souls. In Palestine, in biblical times, a farmer would sow seed after the early rains, which prepared the soil for the seed. The latter showers of spring refreshed and accelerated the ripening harvest, yielding a bumper crop. This passage connects a coming mighty harvest that Jesus is patiently waiting to have an outpouring of His Spirit on the earth.

Myth #5—People are tired of the gospel; nobody wants to hear it.

Surveys show that most Americans claim to be more open to spiritual things now than at almost any other time in history. This is true of the nations as well. In a recent poll, Jesus was chosen by the majority of people as the person they would most want to spend time with out of all the historical figures.

Do you not say, "There are still four months and then comes the harvest"? Behold, I say to you, lift up your eyes and look at the fields, for they are already white for harvest! (John 4:35)

God is saying the harvest is always ripe. The deficiency is only with the laborers; the laborers are few. The harvest is always ripe and it doesn't matter where you are geographically; the promise is not discriminating. There's a field white for harvest in even the most difficult places.

For in this the saying is true: "One sows and another reaps." I sent you to reap that for which you have not labored; others have labored, and you have entered into their labors (John 4:37-38).

92

God sent us to do a job and we're going to reap because He is the one who sent us to do it! When we launch out at His Word, we're going to catch what we need to catch. We've been released in divine authorization to reap, even in some instances where we've not labored. He didn't send you out to come back empty-handed, He sent you to reap!

Myth #6—America isn't a Christian nation anymore.

A flash point is a point at which something or someone bursts suddenly into action or being. God's Church will always be the flash point of whether or not God moves in the nation. God's movement is not based on the forces arrayed against His purposes, but on the hearts aligned with His purposes.

Believing that we once were one thing and then it was taken away, gives us the mentality that our best days are behind us. No, our best days are yet to come! People are in need, regardless of their nation's direction, and God is resolute in His redemptive agenda.

CHAPTER 5

HEARTBROKEN FOR HUMANITY

*"This generation of believers
is responsible for this generation of souls."*
—Keith Green

IT WAS 1990 AND I HAD JUST GOTTEN MARRIED. I was watching a show on CNN about a report at Chico, California, of a week of riotous partying by college students. At that time, Chico State University was called "the number one party school" by *Playboy* magazine. The TV report was showing kids completely out of control throwing Molotov cocktails, bouncing cars, with mobs going down the street.

I remember thinking, "Whoever goes there has to be out of their mind!" As I was watching this, a student stood up in the midst of it all and I suddenly felt the burden to go there. Even though my wife and I were married only three months, we moved to Chico. We hardly knew anyone there.

On the first Monday I got out on the campus, I really didn't feel any passion. I felt out of my element. I went there Tuesday. Nothing. I went there Wednesday. Nothing. I said to my wife, "Babe, maybe we missed it and I shouldn't have moved you out here." But she encouraged me and said, "Let's give it more time."

I went back Thursday. It was just about 12:00 noon and I was sitting on the ledge of the quad and all of a sudden, the clock struck. As it chimed, the students came pouring into the quad. I was stuck as

95

thousands of kids just stood there around me. As I looked up at the crowd, they ceased to be a faceless mass. They began to be the very intention of why God had sent His Son. For some unexplained reason I just began to weep profusely.

I was making a scene as I felt God's overwhelming love for them. I had to find a place to release this burden, so I walked down the street to my car. I sat there in my car, hitting my dashboard and saying, "God, You've got to save these students. Whatever You've got to do in my life, do it."

I felt like God spoke to me this verse (see John 12:24), "Unless a grain of wheat falls into the ground and dies, it remains alone; but if it dies, it produces much grain." God's challenge to me was did I care enough about these students and was I willing to lay my life down. In that moment I said, "Yes, Lord," and I felt like God said, "Okay, then I can move through you."

On the Chico University campus, we started seeing people getting saved left and right. But I believe the real turning point came when I was able to become heartbroken for humanity.

A PLAGUE HAS BEGUN

In Numbers 16, Moses and Aaron model for prophetic evangelists what it means to be broken and moved with compassion. They face a similar situation to what you and I face today.

Now it happened, when the congregation had gathered against Moses and Aaron, that they turned toward the tabernacle of meeting; and suddenly the cloud covered it, and the glory of the Lord appeared. Then Moses and Aaron came before the tabernacle of meeting. And the Lord spoke to Moses, saying, "Get away from among this congregation, that I may consume them in a moment." And they fell on their faces. So Moses said to Aaron, "Take a censer and put fire in it from the altar, put incense on it, and take it quickly to the congregation and make atonement for them; for wrath has gone out from the Lord. The plague has begun." Then Aaron took it as Moses commanded, and ran into the midst of the assembly; and already the plague had begun among the people. So he put in the incense and made atonement for the people. And he stood between the dead and the living; so the plague was stopped (Numbers 16:42-48).

The Bible says that the people had gathered against Moses. Moses represented the law. He represented God's ways and purposes. We see a nation of people that had gathered against God's purposes and His laws. We see that in our world today—a plague has begun.

The definition of a plague is "a blow, a striking, and a stumbling."

Haven't we had that in our world today? We've had all three. There's been a striking against God's Word, the name of God, and His righteousness. As a result of this striking there has also come a stumbling. Our world stumbles over what is right and wrong.

As the story goes, a plague hit because the people had turned and gathered themselves against Moses. Aaron had the choice to remain safe back in the church house. Francis Schaeffer, the great Christian thinker, predicted that the greatest threat to the cause of Christ would be if we became a nation filled with Christians whose goal in life was personal peace and prosperity.

The people of Israel had been disobedient to God, so now a plague had hit the nation. Aaron stood there, looking out from the temple at the chaos. He could see the people dying, as the plague was going right through the nation. In this crucial moment, Aaron did something so mighty—he ran in the midst of them. Aaron had to break out. He probably thought to himself, "I can't just stay back at the nice temple looking out as people are dropping like flies out there. If this plague is breaking out, I need to break out too!"

Aaron went and lit a censer and began to make atonement. That's intercession; when one begins to cry out for the people. Aaron ran down among the people. At this time, Aaron is well beyond modern-day retirement age, nevertheless this guy picks up his long priestly garment, and he sprints out there. The burdened heart of the prophetic evangelist says, "I will either live with the living or die with the dying, but I've got to do something."

The single greatest need for Christianity is for us to have what Aaron had in that moment: the explosive compassion that says, "I'm going to run out in the midst. I'm going to stand with the living and the dead."

97

We've got to see the gospel in its highest terms. The gospel is nothing less than what saves a nation. The gospel is what stops a plague. What Aaron did to stop the plague is legendary. We are given "gap principles" for interceding as prophetic evangelists.

Practical instructions for standing in the gap:

1. Recognize the infection. It is only as we see the effects that sin has on people that we will contend with compassion. Sometimes we will witness the hurt they've experienced, and at other times we will feel the harm they release. Each instance is evidence that we can't just stand by and watch. Jesus, in Matthew 9:35-38, when He saw the crowd, was gripped with compassion. The dynamic was achieved, because He got around hurting people and their oppression registered. There is a fresh need to get around the lost until it registers and we recognize the infection.

2. Seek to be covered. Anytime we step out to war for souls, it's vitally important that we are connected to a local body and covered by His presence. If we're not properly related to a local church, we will be unable to adequately function in what it takes to be a lifeline for the lost, and it becomes easy to develop shortsighted tendencies and be more vulnerable to attacks.

When darkness covered the people, the ministers of God looked to be covered by the cloud. There used to be a popular phrase, "I got you covered," meaning that where you would be lacking, someone would help in that place of shortcoming. When you set out to respond in compassion to the spiritually bankrupt, God will cover you if you'll turn to Him.

As Moses and Aaron recognized the infection, they turned toward the tabernacle. Prophetic evangelists know that they must have a positive posture towards God's house. They also realize their insufficiency and vulnerability apart from being clothed in God's manifest presence. If you turn to God to be equipped, He will release His glory upon you.

3. Get lit up. The act of putting fire in your censer might be the most pivotal. I'm convinced that a true burden of the Lord will drive us to fire. There's no excuse for a fireless censer in the desperate hour we live. No fire—no effect. In the Old Testament, priests were told to keep the fire burning (see Lev. 6:13). Isaiah prophesies, "The filth of the people would be purged by the spirit of judgment and by the spirit of burning" (Isa. 4:4). The spirit of burning is an invigorating anointing that makes people zealously affected in a good work. It is an ardent love to Christ that carries you on with resolve in a burden for souls. Fire is the guarantee of divine assistance and the heavenly fuel necessitated.

4. Enter into intercession. When Aaron was told to make atonement for the people, to appropriate the atonement, the tool the Father gave was intercession. Isaiah affirms that Christ, our example, "made intercession for the transgressors" (Isa. 53:12). This is the pattern prophetic evangelists must follow with passion. In this passage Isaiah also states that Jesus was numbered with the transgressors. These two concepts speak of our assignment to identify with the unchurched, and love enough to stand in the gap. Our intercession, like Aaron's, will make a difference. God is still looking for those who will stand in the gap and partner to release God's purposes in the earth.

Oh, that my head were waters, and my eyes a fountain of tears, that I might weep day and night for the slain of the daughter of my people! (Jeremiah 9:1)

Jeremiah's desire was that he would have more tears to cry for the people. He was contending with compassion, just as Aaron did. For Jeremiah, the thoughts of the perished constantly entered his consciousness. He held these pictures in his mind day and night. This can become our model for intercession.

5. Stand in the battlefield. After Aaron prepared himself, the Bible says, "He ran into the midst," and "stood between the living and the dead." Being heartbroken for humanity moves us into the marketplace where we step into the lives of the perishing, willing to put ourselves on the line, where we no longer avoid "sinners" or "sinner hangouts." We stand wherever and whenever God calls us. Aaron responded with his heart and hastened to make a difference. He saw the bodies falling to the plague and went to the root of the problem. Aaron didn't return until the mission was accomplished.

Our assignment is to love people enough to endure the challenges that stand in the way of their conversion.

ROUSED FROM YOUR ROUTINE

In 1996, I was on staff at a church in Southern California. It was my date night with my wife. I was finishing up my work and looking at the clock: 4:30, 4:45, 4:50. I was getting excited to take my wife out for a dinner. 5:00! I grabbed my stuff and headed out to the parking lot.

As I got closer to my car I could see this man in the distance and I could tell there was something wrong with him. I remember thinking, "Oh God, don't let this guy walk up to me; it's my date night!"

As soon as I said that, the guy walks right up to me and asks, "Are you a pastor at this church?" I said, "Yes," but I wanted to say, "I'm occupied right now." Just as I was going to make a similar excuse, he said, "I want you to give me one reason why I shouldn't kill myself. I'm going to give you one chance to talk me out of it, and if you don't, I'm going to end it all."

I started to think of all the lines that I use when I go to witness to someone, but I felt a little bit of pressure. He also got upset whenever I said the name of Jesus. He said, "You think I'm playing?" He reached in his car and grabbed a gun and set it down on the other side of him, but right by me.

Then the man says, "If you don't give me a good reason, I'm not only going to kill myself, but I'm going to kill you first!" I asked him what his name was and what was going on. His name was Rocky and he started telling me, "I'm just mad."

Then Rocky said, "Just talk, man!" I started quickly saying, "Hold on, hold on. Jesus Christ changed my life and He can make a difference in your life too." Every time I would mention Jesus, he would cut me off. He started opening up by telling me he had been abused by his dad. His dad was an alcoholic and was abusive to him and his mother. While I was listening, I could smell alcohol on his breath.

He went on to tell me that when he got older, he had joined the Navy Seals where the training was pretty intense. But he had gotten kicked out with a Dishonorable Discharge. One of his Navy Seals buddies had hit him and Rocky had beaten him within an inch of his life. Later on, he married a young gal who contracted cancer and died in his arms, so now he was drunk, widowed, had an abusive past, and was ready to end it all.

I kept trying to witness to him, but he kept getting more agitated. He grabbed his gun and I said, "Hey, hey, Rocky, let me buy you something to eat at this delicatessen. They've got great sandwiches." He reluctantly went with me. We got in my car with his gun still on him. He ordered corned beef on rye. I then decided that I wasn't going to have anything because (a) this might be my last meal, and (b) I suddenly felt led to fast at that moment.

I really felt frustrated because I wasn't having any success with Rocky. But the one thing I hadn't done up to that point was pray; I hadn't asked God to join in. So as I prayed and blessed the food, I threw in, "God, I pray that You will help Rocky."

When I finished the prayer, he pushed the food away and asked, "What did you just do?" When he first looked at me, I thought I had done something wrong. But Rocky said, "When you started to pray, I felt a Hand touch me on the top of my head and went all the way down my neck and my spine. I don't know what it is, but something is telling me I need to let you pray with me."

We prayed and he gave his life to Jesus Christ, and I was able to submit his name for follow up. The significant thing about this incident is that it was no longer about my plans and what I wanted to pursue once I recognized that this was life or death to this guy. For me to take some extra time out of my day meant all the difference in the world.

DEFINING A BURDEN

A prayer burden is a deep desire on the heart of God that is imparted by the Holy Spirit to someone whose intercession the Holy Ghost desires to use.

Jesus has been interceding for the needs of the lost, and now the Spirit needs you to join with the intercession of Jesus. Before evangelism is a program, it is a passion—a passion of the heart, which brings in saving action. Evangelism is the passion of Moses. "Oh, this people have sinned...yet now, if You would forgive them—if not, blot me, I pray, out of the book which You have written."

PROPHETIC EVANGELISM

It is the passion of Paul, "Woe is me if I preach not the gospel." It is the anguished cry of Jesus as He wept over a doomed city, "O Jerusalem, how much I long to gather you." Passion is the cry of John Knox, "Give me Scotland or I die," and of John Wesley, "The world is my parish." Evangelism passion is Henry Martyn landing on the shores of India and crying, "Here let me burn out for God!" It is David Brainerd coughing up blood from tuberculosis as he prays in the snow for the early Native Americans. It is George Whitefield crossing the Atlantic 13 times in a small boat to preach in the American Colonies.
"Oh Lord, give me souls or take my soul."
—George Whitefield

ATTRIBUTES OF A BURDEN

1. A burden is spiritual engagement. It is a desire for God's mercy and help for that which is highest and best for an individual. This concern weighs down upon the praying person, causing that one to pray as much as possible for the need.

2. A burden is of divine origin. Its source is not natural sympathy or emotions. It is not something worked up by the flesh; it is born in the heart of God and conveyed to you by the Spirit's guidance.

3. A burden is individually unique. Others may not share your vision, burden, or concern. But if God has laid it upon you, you're still responsible to intercede.

4. A burden is deeply impressionable. When the Lord places the burden upon you heavily, it literally weighs upon your heart. The more fully you identify with the need, the more deeply you will feel it.

5. A burden makes you accountable. A Spirit-given burden is a special mandate from the Lord. You may be the only one to whom the Spirit assigns this prayer burden.

COMPASSION OF CHRIST

The critical nature of sin moved God to go from Heaven to earth to administer a cure: Jesus Christ had to die on a cross. The Lamb was slain before the foundation of the world (see Rev. 13:8).

102

Jesus wrote the script on how He would die. A script that said He would be betrayed by a friend; that He would be scoffed and mocked; that many of the people who had cheered Him on would be the same ones who cheered for Him to be crucified; that He would be punched, beaten, whipped, and crucified in the most excruciatingly painful way.

Don't you think this is One who understands the seriousness of sin and the measure that has to be taken to get the Cure out to everyone? After accomplishing all that was prophesied for Him to do, He left a mission for all of those who would follow Him.

Just before the upper room, the disciples were given the Great Commission. There was an explosion as their lives became bent on releasing the power of the gospel message. The word *redemption* comes from the Hebrew word "to tear loose and to rescue." That's what we do! We rip the person out of the hold of sin and rescue them.

The Bible often declares that people who are not saved are seen as captives of any array of forces: sin, sickness, satan, and death. It has laid an illegitimate claim on humanity. Jesus described lost people as captives held in a deadly grip.

Jesus had purpose statements. His mission was to seek and save the lost. There is a love and a vengeance in His mission. Think of satan's surprise on that day when Jesus said, "It is finished." In utter horror, he looks up and recognizes, in that moment, that God so loved people who were alienated from Him, that He would bankrupt all of Heaven to send His best—His Son Jesus Christ.

My soul breaks with longing; for Your judgments at all times (Psalm 119:20).

If you want to understand God, He is a "redemptocentric." He has a heart fixed on searching for the lost. His heart is all about rescuing and delivering. The ultimate oppression is the ignorance that keeps people from knowing Jesus.

The crucial characteristic that brings about your greatest "success" in helping others is having the heart of Father God. You will be a rescuer if you can close your eyes in prayer and see the faces of lost people, knowing that hell is real and they have to get to Heaven. Believers need to see it as a real place—get connected with the Commission.

LOSTOLOGY

Lostology is about understanding lost people and loving lost people by giving them directions to God.

Think about being lost on a road somewhere. If you're driving to a new place and realize you're lost, are you going to get directions by calling someone you have a relationship with? It's awkward enough when you're lost, so you like to talk to someone you know. Sometimes God puts people into your life for the purpose of having a "redemptive relationship." Don't be afraid to use the collateral you've invested in a relationship by doing the most important thing you can ever do for someone—give them Jesus. If Jesus has made a difference in your life, then you ought to tell somebody about it!

We don't like to admit we're lost, do we? We know how it feels to not know where we are. We have to learn how to be relevant to this generation.

SPIRITUAL A.D.D.
—AGAPE DEFICIT DISORDER

The Bible says in Matthew 24:12, on account of lawlessness, the hearts of many will grow cold. I think there are degrees of what it means to be cold. There can be a self-righteous coldness where a numbness towards the condition of the world sets in.

There has been a modern Christian viewpoint where there is a tendency to have a hardness toward people. Jonah was a unique prophet who saw one of the largest revivals in the Old Testament. I believe there is a mind-set called "the Jonah Syndrome."

Now the word of the Lord came to Jonah the son of Amittai, saying, "Arise, go to Nineveh, that great city and cry out against it; for their wickedness has come up before Me" (Jonah 1:1-2).

The Ninevites were known as being ruthless and wicked and here God says, "Go to Nineveh, that great city." Now that was generous. One of the worst things to get stuck on is how wicked your city is. When people talk about how wicked all of the major cities in the U.S. are, it just sucks all of the faith and hope out of people. But God sees cities from a redemptive angle! Part of having the heart of God is having His eyes. He sees people as what they could be, not what they are.

THE JONAH SYNDROME

Jonah's slant was convenience. The major thing that is an enemy of receiving a burden of the Lord is that we live in a culture that worships convenience. We drive past restaurants and they throw our food through the window. We push buttons on our computers to replace shopping. The word *convenience* means "absence of trouble, attuned to one's personal comfort, and ease of action." Jonah didn't want to go to Nineveh; he wanted to go to Tarshish, which was a totally different place from Nineveh. It was like he was taking off on a vacation to leisure world. He wanted to do his own thing.

Having the burden of the Lord is not about convenience. If you're going to look at the true Christian life, it is not going to be convenient for you. The fact is, dying on a cross is not convenient. Jesus could have just said, "Father, save Me from this hour." But no, He said, "For this very purpose I have come into the world." He chose to fulfill His destiny to be the Deliverer.

You are a part of a people God has produced to penetrate the veil of the ordinary. You are a golden, holy storehouse of God's potential. You have the life in you to liberate literally the entire world. You've got enough gospel truth in you to see a full-fledged "God move" shape your nation overnight. A fresh release of mercy is much needed in this hour. What sabotaged Jonah's leisure trip was actually God's move of mercy. God sent a big fish to get Jonah so he would be a fisher of men.

Those who regard worthless idols; forsake their own mercy (Jonah 2:8).

This verse also uses the term "lying vanities" for worthless idols, describing the deceptive smoke screens of all the spiritual substitutes. Do you know what the sabotage of a burden is? It's being distracted by entertainment and personal goals that are not necessarily God's plan for us.

O Jerusalem, Jerusalem, the one who kills the prophets and stones those who are sent to her! How often I wanted to gather your children together, as a hen gathers her chicks under her wings, but you were not willing! (Matthew 23:37)

Human nature would say it's okay to be offended over their behavior, but no, Jesus said in spite of that He still wants to gather them together because He loves them. The only thing that's stopping us is that we won't let His love move in us.

There's something deeper than political persuasions, affiliations, and social causes; it's the ultimate sense that we are a part of the offspring of God. We are the kingdom of God. Our greatest affiliation must be that we are lovers of Christ and deliverers of people.

Whatever else you are and whatever else you identify with, you must be, above all, a follower of Christ.

ETERNAL BODY SNATCHING

The prophet Joel speaks of how imperative a broken heart realization is, in the repairing of broken lives.

The seed shrivels under the clods, storehouses are in shambles; barns are broken down, for the grain has withered (Joel 1:17).

In this passage a picture is given about the gospel remaining locked in unbroken hearts. The seed represents the gospel message, and the clods represent unbroken hearts. The storehouse speaks of churches, and the barns could represent our communities. Finally, the grain is an image of the harvest. The final picture becomes a tragic view that cities and communities break down because believers won't break down. Today's evangelism makes tomorrow's harvest possible.

The spiritual capital invested in our generation by previous generations of believers will eventually be exhausted. We must be new "brokers" of spiritual wealth for our nation.

Do you not say, "There are still four months and then comes the harvest"? Behold, I say to you, lift up your eyes and look at the fields, for they are already white for harvest! And he who reaps receives wages, and gathers fruit for eternal life, that both he who sows and he who reaps may rejoice together. For in this the saying is true: "One sows and another reaps." I sent you to reap

106

that for which you have not labored; others have labored, and you have entered into their labors (John 4:35-38).

A big church is not an end in itself—it's an instrument for evangelism. God makes it big to have a big impact, but the water ripples are expected to go further.

When I was a kid I can remember seeing a horror movie classic that shook me up—it still shakes me up! It was called "*Invasion of the Body Snatchers*." There was an alien intergalactic enemy that planted parasitical organisms called "pods." These "pods" would make an alien clone substitute of you while you were sleeping, leaving a shell of who you were and the clone of you would have the alien's agenda.

People found out about it and heroically tried to thwart the aliens and rescue folks. My buddies and I would cover our eyes every time the pod would shoot out vines, which mutated people during slumbering times. It was frightening, and anxiety would fill our bodies. I've often thought about this movie since then and can feel my pulse rise thinking about those pods. This movie plot was not as original as I thought. This same plot is described in Matthew 13:24-28.

The kingdom is likened to a man who sowed good seed, and while he slept, his enemy sowed tares, which originally looked like wheat. Tares were false plants that resembled the true, but tares impede the wheat's maturity. In the movie, to save folks, you had to do two things:

1. Wake them before it was too late, and
2. Rip off the false vines connected to them that mutated its host.

Today, the enemy wants to mutate the Body of Christ. He plants substitute agendas, cloned programs, and tangential emphasis that impede evangelism taking place through churches. Our adversary wants to replace God's soul-winning agenda in you. Churches who don't have evangelistic outreach have signed their own death certificates. We must wake up and rip off of us all of the false vines trying to mutate us from being the soul-winning organisms that we are called to be.

It is vital that you, as a Christian, be dedicated to sharing your faith and maintaining your motivation in the face of persecution. To not preach the gospel means you hide the medicine for the patient who is dying.

THREE REVELATIONS THAT WILL KEEP YOU MOTIVATED IN BODY SNATCHING:

1. A revelation of hell—Luke 16:24

When the rich man, who had no time for the things of God during his life, gets a major glimpse of hell, he suddenly became evangelistic.

2. A revelation of rewards—Luke 16:9

What we need is a revelation of the value of a soul. What Jesus is saying in this verse is if you'll use your money to get people saved, when you die they are going to be there waiting to receive you in Heaven.

3. A revelation of the stockpile factor—2 Kings 7:7-9

One of the strongest motivations of all is a realization of the abundant provision we have in Christ.

In Second Kings 6, the four lepers recognized that their discovery of abundant blessing must be followed up with delivering that "good news" to others. It says in Daniel 12:3, "Those who are wise shall shine like the brightness of the firmament. And those who turn many to righteousness like the stars forever and ever."

ACTION STEP ADDENDUM
A FRESH BAPTISM OF BROKENNESS

It says in the Bible that we have this treasure in earthen vessels (see 2 Cor. 4:7-12). Spiritual effectiveness lies in God coming out through us. I want to extend a lifeline to lost humanity, and the question is, how do I let this lifeline come out through me? How do I get the life that is in me out of me in order to reach others? A clue to this is addressed by classic author T.A. Sparks. He wrote, "As an instrument, the soul has to be won, mastered, and ruled in relation to the higher ways of God."

There is something that has to do with our soul that helps the treasure and life on the inside to be able to get out. The Church is designed by God to be a prophetic influence on every other sphere in the earth, which is why this revelation is so paramount.

1. Brokenness releases the treasure. In the one who is unbroken, the gospel is blocked and can't flow out. Brokenness releases the treasure within you. Is it possible that the reason 95 percent of Christians have never led a soul to Christ is because we've gone through our Christian walk unbroken?

If you have an unbroken heart, your spirit is unable to function, or it comes forth mixed with your own thoughts and emotions. This works in every relationship in your life. Brokenness is a weapon. If I can become broken, something within me can get outside of me and touch someone else, and when my spiritual life touches their spiritual death, they're awakened. Spirit doesn't touch spirit if you're not broken.

2. Brokenness brings revelation. Jesus always had the right words, because He knew men's hearts. The more broken you are the more sensitive you are. How many of you can hear God so much clearer after you have had a good cry at the altar?

When I'm broken, my discernment is really on. Our effectiveness is closely related to our discernment of people's spiritual conditions. When I'm not broken, I can be full of distracting preoccupations. I'm convinced that if you are broken when you pray for folks, you will be able to discern exactly what is going on with them because the Word of God rises up inside of a broken person. Our spirit is released according to the degree of our brokenness.

Brokenness is a state of heart. Whenever we preserve and make excuses for ourselves we're deprived of spiritual sensitivity and supply.

Prophetic evangelism is about spirit touching spirit. It isn't about merely giving head knowledge to somebody in hopes of reaching them.

When your spirit touches another spirit, God awakens the spirit that has darkness in it. They may choose to harden themselves, but it's a serious fight on their part when spirit touches spirit. The whole hunger for spirituality that's in the world today is simply a craving for spirit to touch spirit.

Divine prescriptions flow when the walls of the outer man and the inner man are broken down and are no longer contrary. When there is unity between that outward man and that inward man, brokenness allows there to be an accurate diagnosis of situations. Christ's ministry through us is possible to the degree that we are broken. Brokenness—it tears down the walls and releases a pure spirit.

In Second Chronicles 34:27, God said to Josiah, "Because your heart was tender I'm going to show grace before your eyes for your entire life, judgment will be stayed off." Because Josiah was broken he was a blessing to his nation his entire life.

3. Brokenness attracts the lost. Revivalist Evan Roberts had a brokenness that released an atmosphere about him. This atmosphere was attractive to the unreached. The sound that attracts Heaven is the sound of a heart breaking. Roberts saw 110,000 souls come to Christ in one year. Why? Because when Evan Roberts got touched by God, this was his prayer, "O Lord, bend me, bend the Church, save the world!"

Evan Roberts's cry was one of brokenness, abandonment, and total submission. It was said of him that something melted his whole being and a revelation of Calvary's love hit him like never before, and that became the theme of the whole revival. It was also cited that he carried the ability to usher in the presence of the Holy Spirit as almost a tangible force.

The open door to having God's presence is preceded by lamenting, mourning, and weeping. Mourning produces a dynamic necessary to be receptive to what God reveals and a receptacle of what God releases (see James 4:9-10). Brokenness pulls the trigger on releasing what God has invested inside of us.

STEPS TO PULLING THE TRIGGER

1. Ask the Holy Spirit to pour God's love into your heart.
2. Seek to be broken by God's compassion.
3. Identify with the needs of lost humanity.
4. Begin to cry out for the unsaved trapped in darkness.
5. Become a lifeline for those who need hope.

Now that we hit the dynamic of brokenness, I want to give you 15 areas for you to pray for your lost loved ones:

15 KEY INTERCESSORY TARGETS

1. Pray that God would draw them to Himself, as only He can do—John 6:44.
2. Pray they seek to know God—Acts 17:26-27.
3. Pray they believe the Word of God—First Thessalonians 2:13.
4. Pray that satan is kept from blinding them from the truth—Second Corinthians 4:4.
5. Ask the Holy Spirit to convict them of their sin, and their need for Christ's redemption—John 16:8-13.
6. Ask for God to soften their hearts—Hebrews 3:15.
7. Ask God to send someone who will share the gospel with them—Matthew 9:37-38.
8. Ask God to loose laborers for the harvest—Matthew 9:38.
9. Pray that God would give you the opportunity, the courage, and the right words to be able to share the truth with them—Colossians 4:2-6 and Ephesians 6:18-20.
10. Pray they turn from their sin and the error of their ways—Acts 17:30-31 and First Thessalonians 1:9-10.
11. Ask God to open their eyes—Second Corinthians 4:3-4.
12. Pray they would put all their trust in Christ—John 1:12; 5:24.
13. Ask that God will loose the ministry of angels—Hebrews 1:13-14.
14. Pray they make Jesus Christ the Lord of their life—Romans 10:9-11.
15. Ask that they take root and grow in their faith—Second Corinthians 2:6-7.

"My one ambition in life is to win as many as possible.
Oh, it is the only thing worth doing, to save souls."
—R.A. Torrey

CHAPTER 6

COMING OUT WITH THE BIG GUNS

IF WE'RE GOING TO WIN SOULS, we're going to have to war. But the challenge will be to outlast and outrun the opposition in this last hour. There is a problem in the Church today. I believe that problem is that we don't know how to be a channel for the raw power of God. We don't know how to let God flow through us the way He wants to. A channel is a tube that water flows through, or a conduit that electricity flows through. We need the water of the Spirit and the electrical dynamo of the Holy Ghost to flow through us in new dimensions.

When I read the Book of Acts, the Church didn't have this problem. When you have a power shortage in the Body of Christ, you're left to relying upon man-made things. Today, we're often left to synthetic solutions when the answers to our problems are supernatural. Now is not the time to handle it on our own!

Let's look at two consequences of not knowing how to properly channel the Spirit:

1. We are not seeing an overcoming, empowered people as God designed us to be. Jesus died on the cross so you and I could be totally empowered people. When our testimony is anything less than that overcoming level, it casts a negative light on what Christianity represents to the world.

2. We are not attracting the world's attention because we appear too often to live a contradiction to our message. We say, "Come to Christ and He will break your addictions and He will deliver you from bondage." Yet, when we look at our current state, we also have all the problems that we are proclaiming Jesus will set people free from.

SPIRITUAL WEAPONS OF MASS DESTRUCTION

We are coming against the "big guns." You're not having little attacks come against you; you are having full blown, three-alarm trials come upon you. You and I may wish that our warfare would be lighter, yet much of it is due to the times we live in.

Now as Jannes and Jambres resisted Moses, so do these also resist the truth: men of corrupt minds, disapproved concerning the faith; but they will progress no further, for their folly will be manifest to all, as theirs also was (2 Timothy 3:8-9).

The end-time Church is going to experience the facing off of the big guns. Jannes and Jambres were the New Agers of Pharaoh's court. They tapped into the dark, demonic powers performing lying signs and wonders. Paul tells us what is going to happen in the last days. He declares in this verse that the big guns are coming out. The battle lines are not drawn over ideologies as much as spiritual forces.

The second thing that happens when we properly channel the Spirit is that the end-time Church will experience what Moses experienced. Moses took a rod in his hand and released a noticeable authority over Jannes and Jambres. I believe that the end-time Church is going to receive a rod of supernatural power, where miracles will become the order of the day. I want to see the supernatural power of God, yet it is so easy to tie into today's culture that is so cynical. We almost don't want to extend ourselves to believe!

Paul is saying that what Moses experienced, we're going to experience. This means that we're going to come with a similar power in the endtimes. Isn't that exciting?

The advancing influence of false prophetic powers and dark spiritual forces will come to a sudden stop. They will be cut off, illustrated by the fact that verse 9 says, "They will progress no further, for their folly will be manifest to all."

Paul is saying that this will include all dark supernatural forces, including witchcraft. Witchcraft is to power for non-believers, what the

Holy Ghost is to power for believers. The Bible uses the Greek word *dunamis*, which means, "dynamite, explosive, miracle power." It's the hour where witchcraft is squaring off against dunamis.

It's that element where the anointing of whatever source you're plugged into will prove to be your destiny. This means that we are going to demonstrate power that will override the sorcery that is coming up against us.

> *Now when they had gone through the island to Paphos, they found a certain sorcerer, a false prophet, a Jew whose name was Bar-Jesus, who was with the proconsul, Sergius Paulus, an intelligent man. This man called for Barnabas and Saul and sought to hear the word of God. But Elymas the sorcerer (for so his name is translated) withstood them, seeking to turn the proconsul away from the faith. Then Saul, who also is called Paul, filled with the Holy Spirit, looked intently at him and said, "O full of all deceit and all fraud, you son of the devil, you enemy of all righteousness, will you not cease perverting the straight ways of the Lord? And now, indeed, the hand of the Lord is upon you, and you shall be blind, not seeing the sun for a time." And immediately a dark mist fell on him, and he went around seeking someone to lead him by the hand. Then the proconsul believed, when he saw what had been done, being astonished at the teaching of the Lord* (Acts 13:6-12).

Acts 13 is a turning point. Winston Churchill would call it an "unhinged moment in history." The apostle Paul is about to have a battle that changes him from Saul to Paul because he walked in the Spirit. It changed his identity, and one battle can change your identity too!

YOU CAN RUN, BUT YOU WON'T GROW

The worst thing you and I can do is run from our spiritual battles. God wants to transform us and He does this in the midst of our battles. Just one battle can elevate your anointing, and one battle can get you in where you weren't in before. Don't be afraid to take on battles because it is in the time of battles that the supremacy of the kingdom is demonstrated and manifested.

There was a false prophet named Bar-Jesus. Bar-Jesus was also called Elymas. Saul and Barnabas were back in Jerusalem and the Spirit of the Lord came and said, "I want you to send out Saul and Barnabas." We are living in a time where the Holy Spirit must be the Genius of all we do. The truth of the matter is that you and I have to forge a relationship with the person of the Holy Spirit, unlike any other time in our past. So when He speaks to us, we must hear and move as He directs. Isn't it interesting that this guy Elymas is going around calling himself the son of Jesus? But Paul had that "x-ray discernment" and said, "You are not the son of Jesus; you're the son of the devil." Elymas was boasting that he was divine, but really he was demonic. Paul was called an apostle. Notice that up to this point he never functioned as an apostle. It is not enough to have a title; we've got to function in what we've been calling ourselves.

Here is a crisis in Paul's history, but it's a crisis that in a moment of victory changed his identity. We're in a crisis because God wants to change our identity. He wants to bring a revelation and a revolution to how we function. The crisis that you're in right now is an opportunity to change. We have stuck our heads in the sand in some instances, hoping that the big bad wolf would just go away (or at least quit huffing and puffing). This isn't going to happen. We must be walking in authority and functioning as a victorious Church!

Paul and Barnabas were sent to the island of Paphos by the Holy Spirit. *Paphos* means "boiling hot." This was a hot spot, a war zone, and this place is where the big guns were going off. This is their first missionary trip and they had no idea they would immediately have a hearing with the governor!

The temple of Venus was in Paphos. Venus was worshiped through sexual rites. She was worshiped as queen of Paphos. Literally, her shrine had such a demonic charge on it that one scholar actually wrote, "Neither man nor woman could look at this shrine without being defiled in their minds, and depraved in their character."

How would you like your first missionary trip to be in a place like this? Typically, we send the "veteran" missionaries to the spiritual "danger zones." Paul is sent on his first mission's trip to a place where perversion reigns. He is also given a divine appointment with a

Roman-appointed governor who had a demonized advisor (using false prophetic gifts) by his side. When we look at our world today, is that not the case also? Pornography is a multibillion-dollar business. Psychic advisors are in high demand and are fully "bank rolled."

Here is the key of this whole thing. The Bible says that Paul was "filled with the Holy Spirit." He would not be effective in a place where there was such a demonic stronghold, and a "wreck-you-for-life" statue—unless he was filled with the Spirit of God.

HOW TO BREAK FALSEHOOD

Miraculous manifestations will always be used by God to break the spell of falsehood. You don't break falsehood by debating it, so Paul didn't get into a debate with Elymas. He discerned and dealt with the root issues. Paul flowed in the gift of discernment of spirits, which is the God-given ability to discern the source of a spiritual manifestation, whether it is human, divine, or demonic. As a result, Paul broke through to total liberation for himself and those he ministered to.

> But they will progress no further, for their folly will be manifest
> to all, as theirs also was (2 Timothy 3:9).

The more wicked a place, the more the need for a Spirit-filled witness. The Bible says that the governor was intelligent. We think, "Intelligent people would never get involved in the occult. Intelligent people would never allow themselves to be influenced by witchcraft." Not true. Although he was brilliant, the governor was duped because his advisor was a demonized individual causing a veil of confusion. Paul's approach to intelligence was to flow in the supernatural.

We need the Spirit of God to direct and lead us. All of the intellectuals are praying for one real miracle, and if they see it, many would surrender their lives to God.

In all my years of ministry, I have never seen an intellectual won to Christ with intellectualism. Intellectualism was the wrong tree in the Garden of Eden and it is the wrong tree today. We must study to show ourselves approved, but submit our intellect to the Spirit of God.

Elymas (Bar-Jesus) wanted to maintain control. Demonic powers always want to have control. The greater anointing there is on your life, the greater the attack will be to try to gain control of your life. The greater the opportunity, the greater the opposition. We need to be sitting daily at the fireplace of God's dunamis power saying, "God, give me more."

We're not going to be able to set free a generation who has the spirit of Elymas on them with a nice little sermon about ten reasons why they should listen to me. No, we need the power of God!

THE ELYMAS SPIRIT

Elymas was *skilled in the art of divination*. He was fluent in spiritism and was able to exercise that influence upon others. We have a generation who has been raised on divination in everything from video games to hot lines, from cartoons to daytime talk shows.

Elymas was *a pretender to the gift of prophecy*. He had a counterfeit, which in a vacuum of the real, passed as legitimate. Many spiritists would be out of a job tomorrow if the Church operated in genuine, Holy Spirit gifts and power.

Elymas *perverted the right ways*. This spirit perverts the right ways, so that people don't see what is right. In fact, we have a postmodern generation who says that there is no right. There is no doubt in my mind that there is a spirit of Elymas today. It seeks to misrepresent. He had the ability to put a dark spin on something that would prejudice people's opinion towards Christianity. He could paint anything with false colors.

There's a spirit upon political correctness that is able to put a dark spin and prejudice in the taste buds of a generation. This results in people having built-in biases to the gospel. The Church needs a reformation; we need a change. We need to break the Elymas spirit. Another interesting thing that one scholar said was, "Elymas was a degenerate descendant of the cultic priests of Pharaoh's court." This would tie Elymas to Jannes and Jambres, the Egyptians who opposed Moses, thus fulfilling Paul's prophetic word in Second Timothy 3:8.

CLEAN UP THIS MESS!

I believe that it is going to get messy, but the treasures who come out of darkness are going to be very thrilled and satisfied. We're going to have to loose the grave clothes off of the Lazarus generation coming to us. We're not going to have to make new converts want God. They're going to be so excited to be delivered from being Dracula last week that they're going to be at our churches worshiping God!

In the days to come, the preaching of the gospel is going to produce a different type of opposition. These false spirits are fighting for the same souls we're fighting for, so we have got to be filled with the Holy Spirit! We will have a grace from the Lord to be able to look at people and immediately know how to prescribe what it's going to take to get them out of darkness and into light.

God filled Paul with the Holy Spirit for emergencies just like this. You're going to have some emergencies, so you need to be filled with the Holy Spirit. Paul could repel a sorcerer and attract a governor in one fell swoop. That's prophetic evangelism. In back-to-back verses it says that Saul was filled, and Elymas was filled; what a contrast. Everybody in the coming age of contending for souls will be filled with something.

AWOL OR AWAKE?

A young follower, John Mark, bolted after this scenario. Many scholars have different thoughts on why he might have left. But Paul was very adamant that he wasn't going to take John Mark along with them again. So in Paul's eyes there wasn't an excuse for his absence.

I believe that when John Mark saw that his power encounter got a little messy, he wasn't ready for it, so he bolted. Later on, Barnabas took John Mark with him, and praise God that he did, otherwise we would not have the Gospel of Mark. John Mark went on to write the second book of the Gospels, which focuses on the supernatural nature of Christ. For John Mark, it was the failure of spiritual courage, and it proves that even the best human surroundings will not ensure spiritual steadfastness. Not only did the Spirit send Paul, he was armed by the Spirit. By this power, Paul pronounced a judgment on Elymas that rendered him blind. Elymas was not blind forever, but just for a time. It says that immediately a dark mist fell upon him and he went around seeking someone to lead him.

I don't know what ended up happening to Elymas, but I do know what happened to Sergius Paulus. The Bible says, "The proconsul believed when he saw what had been done."

NEGOTIATING THE OBSTACLE COURSE

Paul's model for evangelism demonstrated that not only did he encounter obstacles, he expected them (see 2 Cor. 7:5). All who want to do the work of the kingdom will encounter some form of plaguing resistance.

Points of Personal Resistance:

1. Fear—Fear is the most common spiritual snag that seizes people. This often manifests itself as nervousness, which handicaps people, defeating them in the locker room before actually witnessing. Failure to recognize this dark spirit, which likes to attach itself to soul winners, results in short-circuiting prophetic leadings, as well as the ability to establish rapport with lost people.

Filling the heart and mind with the greatest fear buster known to mankind (the Word of God) is the answer. When the sword of the Spirit is found in your sheath, you can cut the hindering vines of anxiety! We must remember that God hasn't made us to function with fear, but has released power to us and given us a sound mind to help conquer the fear.

2. Being Misunderstood—In a world where perception is reality, it is easy for the spiritually confused to misinterpret and misconstrue attempts to rescue them. Peter and the boys were misunderstood as being drunk on the Church's birthday and it seems as if mix-ups still get duplicated on a daily basis.

Moses was misunderstood by the Israelites whom he was sent to deliver. They accused him of making things worse and putting a sword in their enemy's hand (see Exod. 5:21). How's that for gratitude? Prophetic evangelists must have "tough skin" and keep their eyes on their callings and their divine goal.

I am often buoyed by the promise God gave Ezekiel the prophet (see Ezek. 3:8-9) when he was told that his forehead was made like "adamant stone, harder than flint." The answer for the clay feet is a flint forehead. God also told Ezekiel not to be dismayed by people's looks.

Sometimes the looks I get when I witness can stump me. Once I realized that I needed God to shine illumination upon souls, I could weather being misunderstood.

3. Discouragement—Discouragement can be so deflating! It's reminiscent of an embedded nail in your new whitewall tire. You just keep losing volume and elevation while being hissed at.

Elijah got discouraged after the miracle of Mt. Carmel, when Ahab and Jezebel weren't convinced or consumed. This feeling can be overwhelming and suffocate the flame of evangelical fervor in a nanosecond.

Many prophets and evangelists have had a bout or two with discouragement. The key to dismissing discouragement is to look to God for our cues and not human expressions.

Your focus means everything in these times. When your focus and courage go, you won't rise up to the demands of the occasion.

4. Doubt and unbelief—Strong feelings of uncertainty and being waylaid by how unlikely someone's salvation seems, is common. If I gave up witnessing every time I've felt doubtful, I wouldn't have seen one person come to Christ, and I wouldn't have stuck around too long.

These twin thieves of doubt and unbelief rob us of a precious harvest and sentence us to watered down expectations. Thomas, the disciple, doubted the testimony of the risen Savior even though he had walked with Jesus for three years and saw His marvels firsthand. He even refused the testimony of his fellow disciples. Yet, Thomas got past this speed bump with Jesus' help and went on to be martyred by pagan priests for preaching the gospel to India. He obviously got through this battle time and time again by touching Jesus.

Touching Jesus is still the antidote to doubt and unbelief. We do this by prayer and worship in time spent alone with God. If we can defeat the unbelief before us, we will defeat the unbelief before them.

5. The devil—He stands to lose the most as souls are won to Christ. There are visible hindrances and invisible hindrances, and what you don't see can be the most lethal. We must not be ignorant of his devices and recognize that this "strong man" is about to be plundered by the Stronger One who lives in you and me. In Luke 11:22, we are told his armor can be taken from him. I'm convinced that this armor involves his limited authority and power, which involves deception.

When we bring light and Christ's authority to trapped hearts, satan's deceptive powers dissipate and we can multiply our converts by dividing the spoil. God is going to ultimately crush satan underneath your "beautiful feet that bring the good news."

BE A VOICE FOR SOULS

Genesis 18 shows us that Abraham was a voice for souls. He cried out and said he would stand in the gap because he was a voice for lost souls in his generation. Remember what he did for Lot and his family? "God, if there are just ten righteous people, don't let judgment come on them."

In Exodus 32, Moses was a voice for souls when Aaron and the people were melting their gold and making idols. "God, if You're going to strike these people, I'm going to stand in the gap." In Esther 8, Esther was a voice for souls. She begged for the lives of her people. "If I die, I die, but I'm going to go before the king and beg on behalf of my people." In Romans 15, the apostle Paul was a voice for souls.

William Booth, the founder of the Salvation Army, would go out to the bars, get people saved, then train and disciple them. Then they would all go out and get people saved. He was quoted to say, "If every Christian could taste hell for 30 minutes, it would be good." If all of us could taste hell, we would be a lot more diligent in soul winning. If we could just relive our lives with all of the oppression before we got saved, we would become a consistent voice for souls.

UNLEASHING INTERCESSION

The secret of reaching men and women is to know the secret of reaching God. The secret of reaching humanity is found in reaching God. We need to unleash intercession for a harvest breakthrough. When we pour out of our spirit in prayer, God pours out of His Spirit in response to our prayer. There needs to be a whole new dimension of intercession. Once I had a vision of a golden ladder (similar to the story of Jacob) where God wanted to begin moving in cities. Angels were ascending up and down the ladders. I knew it meant the free circulation of ministry influence. It reminded me there was a connection between what was going on in the earth and what was going on in Heaven. The enemy works to disconnect us from understanding that connection. He doesn't want us to see that what we do in terms of prayer, and our heart's compassion for the lost, releases things in the heavenlies.

Intercession not only affects who I'm witnessing to, it also releases something in the heavenlies. Whenever I speak the Word and act like Christ, I'm releasing something in the atmosphere.

IT'S VEILED

But even if our gospel is veiled, it is veiled to those who are perishing, whose minds the god of this age has blinded, who do not believe, lest the light of the gospel of the glory of Christ, who is the image of God, should shine on them (2 Corinthians 4:3-4).

The Bible says our gospel is veiled. Unbelievers don't understand because they can't understand. It takes God to reveal God. It takes God to remove the veil.

Lost people don't understand when we share, because they can't understand. Somehow we've got to see that veil. The word "veil" in the Greek is *kalupsis*, and the Greek word for "revelation" is *apokalupsis*. To see the lost converted requires a God-sent revelation to undo the veil. The cover-up is what satan does; the uncovering is what God does. When you're witnessing and you wonder why a person is not getting it, it's because they can't get it apart from apokalupsis. That is why effective witnessing takes prayer.

A COUPLE MORE THOUGHTS

A person hearing the gospel has to have a revelation to see the light, and that is why prayer is so vital. Doing spiritual transactions requires God's removal of the veil. You've got to come against the veil with prayer. You cannot penetrate a spiritual veil with natural weapons. You cannot be witty enough, or say the perfect words, only God can remove this veil. Life will get easier for you when you understand this. I used to get so frustrated in my earlier evangelism days because I was trying to remove a spiritual veil with natural weaponry. Then the Lord set me on a track to pray. I'll be honest. I didn't enjoy prayer. If I felt God's presence with me, it was great, but there were times when it felt uninspired. At those times, it was really a struggle for me, until I began to understand that even when there are no goose bumps, prayer can still be effective, and God will use it. There's a reward in a commitment to prayer, regardless of feelings. Part of the reward of being disciplined in prayer is becoming an influencer and having favor with people.

> *For though we walk in the flesh, we do not war according to the flesh. For the weapons of our warfare are not carnal but mighty in God for pulling down* [change of control and rulership] *strongholds, casting down arguments* [speculations, imaginations, and calculative reasonings] *and every high thing that exalts itself against the knowledge of God, bringing every thought into captivity to the obedience of Christ...* (2 Corinthians 10:3-5).

The context of this passage is not about just doing warfare for you, but doing it on behalf of other people. This spiritual battle is not just dealing with your own thoughts, but dealing with the thoughts in other people. God is saying, "I have empowered you to cast down arguments, belief systems, and reasonings." God has given you heavy-duty artillery to back you up. You have the name and blood of Jesus, and the Holy Spirit to convict. There are even angels working behind the scenes on folks!

Right now you may be thinking, "I'm not good at witnessing," or "I'm too shy." All exploits begin with looking away from our insufficiency and seeing God's sufficiency. We don't generate life, but we release it through prayer!

Satan has a department in hell that works overtime with smear campaigns. He gets you to separate (in your mind) your action from the effect it will produce. Satan wants you to believe that you're wasting your time when you pray. But demons know that when you pray, you can move Heaven and earth! An aspiration will only become a realization with perspiration. Knowing that we're up against the big guns, stirs the prophetic evangelist to get armed and dangerous in the weapons of the Spirit.

SPIRITUAL FASHION SHOW

"No weapon fashioned against you shall prosper" (Isa. 54:17). This verse highlights the fact that the enemy doesn't chuck some indiscriminate weapon in your general direction. He studies you and watches for your tendencies. He knows your strengths and weaknesses. So by the time the weapon leaps out against you, the adversary is confident you will be shut down. Yet Isaiah 54:17 remains as a promise from God which becomes the equalizer in spiritual battles.

While satan is fashioning weapons against us, God is fashioning a defense for us, fashioning you and I into a weapon of choice against the current darkness (see Jer. 51:20). God promises to be our shield (see Ps. 84:9) and to guard and establish us from the evil one (see 2 Thess. 3:3). It is really God, in this hour, who is coming out with the big guns. I want to be an urban Holy Ghost "street sweeper."

Matthew affirms that the kingdom will be taken by the spiritually violent (see Matt. 11:12). Spiritual violence denotes a radical intensity in the inner man to walk in the Spirit no matter what stands in the way. God also fashions a strategy that if we will fall into line with, we will see others rescued and set free into God's purposes.

The strategy of the Lord is made up of two parts. One part is the general redemptive purpose of God to redeem humanity. The second part is a specific assignment for us to step into, which requires an abandonment only found on our knees. When fulfilled, this twofold strategy never fails to see a massive harvest.

Now is your time to do great exploits through the strategy of our Great Commander in Chief, the Lord Jesus Christ.

ACTION STEP ADDENDUM
EMPOWERMENT OF THE SPIRIT

I believe that in this century there will be an inauguration of the "greater works" era for the Body of Christ. Prophetic power will be manifested with a supernatural mantle of gospel-confirming signs. Healing Revivalist, John G. Lake, said, "Christianity is 100 percent supernatural."

One of the single most puzzling enigmas in Scripture is how a small crowd of cowering disciples, jumping at their own shadows, could suddenly metamorphose into a revolutionary army who rocked the early world with the gospel. The answer lies in the dynamic empowerment of the Spirit. The empowerment of the Spirit is so vital to the prophetic evangelist that without supernatural power we will fade into spiritual oblivion. We need this explosive power to fulfill the Great Commission. The Holy Spirit introduces a radically different dimension—a power plant that propels us into another realm of effectiveness.

Definition of Baptism: Being fully covered with. When we are baptized by Christ in the Holy Spirit we become "partakers of the divine nature" at the optimal level.

If you have never been filled with the Holy Spirit, today is your day! I have included steps on how to be empowered by the Spirit. May this empowerment transform your life the way that it has transformed mine.

PRINCIPLES FOR EMPOWERMENT

Jesus knew that we would need both a special boldness and divine "overflow" to be effective prophetic evangelists. The Scriptures teach us that every believer, born of the Word and the Spirit, automatically has the Holy Spirit within. The Holy Spirit came and took up residence in you at the moment of your salvation. We also see in Scripture that the Holy Spirit's empowerment was, in many cases, a subsequent and deliberate step taken by new believers.

The indwelling ministry of the Holy Spirit is automatic; you didn't have to seek His indwelling presence when you first got saved. He came and took up residence within your heart at the moment of your salvation. The empowering of the Spirit is seldom automatic. It usually comes in response to prayer and being proactive about pursuing the empowerment of the Spirit (see Acts 19:2).

If you have never taken this step of faith and experienced the Holy Spirit's filling and empowerment, consider the following points from John 7.

On the last day, that great day of the feast, Jesus stood and cried out, saying, "If anyone thirsts, let him come to Me and drink. He who believes in Me, as the Scripture has said, out of his heart will flow rivers of living water." But this He spoke concerning the Spirit, whom those believing in Him would receive; for the Holy Spirit was not yet given, because Jesus was not yet glorified (John 7:37-39).

1. **"If anyone"**—Accept His invitation to be filled and overflowing with the Spirit.

2. **"Thirsts"**—Express your strong desire to be filled with the Spirit.

3. **"Come to Me"**—Focus on Jesus, believing that He is the one who pours out the Spirit on those who believe.

4. **"Drink"**—Receive by drinking deeply, partaking by faith, of the refreshing and empowering of the Holy Spirit.

5. **"Out of his heart will flow rivers of living water"**—Release the river of the Spirit to flow freely out of your being, bringing life to those thirsty people around you. You release the river by actively ministering to others from the overflow of what you have received.

Definition of Receive—*lambano*: Active; to take with the hand, to seize, to strive to obtain, to take a thing according to agreement.

Being filled with the Holy Spirit is not only a scriptural truth but also an experiential reality. As seen in Scripture, you will know when you have been filled with the Spirit. You will see the effects of this river in your personal life and in a new empowerment to share the good news of Jesus Christ with others!

If this is your desire, I invite you to set aside some time in a quiet place where you can pray this simple prayer to God. When you have finished this prayer, take time to just be alone with Him, simply drinking with gratitude of His empowering Holy Spirit.

"Father, thank You for the gift of forgiveness and eternal life through Jesus Christ Your Son. Jesus is now my Savior and Lord. Having received Your great salvation, I now accept Your invitation to be filled to overflowing with the Holy Spirit. I am asking that Your Spirit would come and satisfy my thirst and become a river of living water pouring out of me. I come to You, believing that You have poured out for me the empowering Holy Spirit. I now, by faith, receive Your empowerment, drinking deeply of You. Fill me with the Holy Spirit now. Let Your Spirit overflow like the river You promised so that others may drink through me. I thank You for this empowerment."

I know that God will honor your desire, thirst, and prayer of faith, sovereignly pouring out the Holy Spirit on you as He did numerous times in Acts.

How to pray for others to receive the empowerment of the Spirit:

1. Teach them what the Bible says about this experience (see Acts 2:1-4).
2. Have them pray and ask God to be filled with the Holy Spirit. Have them confess, worship, and release passionate love towards Christ.
3. Lay your hands on their head and invite the Holy Spirit to fill them.
4. Instruct them to receive what God is doing.
5. When you sense the Holy Spirit upon them, encourage them to express this gift, expecting God's heavenly language and evangelical fervor.

CHAPTER 7

TURNING HEARTS WITH THE ELIJAH ANOINTING

I CAN REMEMBER WHEN WE WERE IN CAMPUS MINISTRY in Northern California, sitting at our tract and book table where we witnessed to people. In the distance, I saw a young man who was running for Student Body President and I immediately saw him through redemptive eyes. I saw him saved and knew that he would be a radical Christian. I walked over and tried to start up a relationship. He blew me off the first time. He was hardened and wanted nothing to do with me.

His fraternity brother had wanted to be a Black Muslim but had given his life to the Lord at an open-air meeting that I had preached at. One day I was discipling the ex-Muslim student and we were talking about the Bible. The young man who was running for Student Body President listened for a while then walked away. A couple of times I would say to him, "God wants to get a hold of your life, man," and he would get upset and walk away. But after about four or five times, he asked me, "Can I talk to you?" I said, "Sure," so we went to KFC and I treated him to some hot wings. While we had sauce all over our fingers, he shared with me that he had fears he could never be faithful to his girlfriend whom he loved.

At that time, he had actually won the presidency, but he was also a male telegram deliverer. I told him that apart from Christ, he couldn't be faithful because he needed the Faithful One to live inside him so he could be faithful. Right there in KFC, I prayed with him and he gave his life to Jesus Christ and was dramatically saved! Later he got baptized in the Holy Ghost. One day he stood up on the free speech lawn at this university. He was such a popular guy (and was the first ethnic minority president at this university) that a great crowd gathered to hear him.

He had previously worn a Playboy bunny medallion around his neck. He took the bunny out of a little box and held it up to everyone and said, "I know you guys have all known me to be this kind of person. This is what I used to be, but it's not what I'm about anymore." He threw the bunny on the ground and reached into his shirt and took out a cross. Then he declared to everyone, "This is what I'm about now. I love Jesus Christ," and he began to share his testimony.

We started to see all kinds of people saved after that. It was a classic example of the Elijah anointing.

PROPHETIC ANOINTING

But if all prophesy, and an unbeliever or an uninformed person comes in, he is convinced by all, he is convicted by all. And thus the secrets of his heart are revealed; and so, falling down on his face, he will worship God and report that God is truly among you (1 Corinthians 14:24-25).

Paul says in First Corinthians 14:24-25 that when there is a prophetic anointing in the midst of a situation, people will feel conviction. When you put the Holy Ghost in the back room and make everything predictable, you're missing the need of a generation.

We need a prophetic anointing. A prophetic anointing is a unique anointing that breaks the junk off of people so they can see their need for Jesus! A prophetic anointing takes you from one place and puts you into another place—just like that. It redefines your identity. This is what you were before, but this is what you're going to be. You may have been bound, but this is how the Lord sees you now. We need the prophetic anointing in evangelism.

The prophetic anointing opens people up to be willing to listen. God intends the prophetic to open a whole new door to evangelism. I believe there is coming a greater prophetic anointing that will open the most hardened place; the most hardened heart. There is going to come a convincing and a conviction that will settle upon lost hearts.

Behold, I will send you Elijah the prophet before the coming of the great and dreadful day of the Lord. And he will turn the hearts of the fathers to the children, and the hearts of the children to their fathers, lest I come and strike the earth with a curse (Malachi 4:5-6).

The prophet Malachi pulls the veil off of the intentions of God to reveal the spirit of Elijah to future generations. This mantle would be released before the second coming and be purposed to take back hearts for God's glory. Historically, Elijah the prophet was best known for rescuing a nation and reviving the name of Yahweh before the eyes of a generation. Elijah's work was to confound the deceptions of his day and vindicate Yahweh's claim to be God alone.

Elijah came upon the scene during a dark time in a nation when other prophets were hiding in caves. The spirit of Jezebel had a stronghold on the hopes of God's people and spiritual confusion was rampant. It was at this moment that God chose to release this secret weapon. Malachi names Elijah as a forerunner. How deep the impression Elijah made on the mind of the nation can be judged by the words of Malachi, which appeared centuries later for the restoration of a nation. Malachi tells of the sending of Elijah as a solution to the problems of separation and alienation.

The significance of the anointing of Elijah is emphasized by the fact that it is called upon in the toughest situations. This is also highlighted in what it accomplishes—hearts are converted! The prophetic anointing, the Elijah anointing, is an anointing that turns hearts. The Bible says in Proverbs 21:1, "The king's heart is in the hand of the Lord, like the rivers of water; He turns it wherever He wishes." Only God is able to turn hearts.

We're dealing with folks today where it's not enough to give them simple, rational proofs; what we call apologetics. I have a friend who ministers on the streets of San Francisco who spoke to two prostitutes. God gave him a word for them. He said to one, "The Lord shows me that when you were eight years old, you were abused and abducted."

She dropped on her knees and lifted up her hands and asked Jesus to help her. Then he turned to the other woman and gave her a word and it had a similar effect.

The prophetic anointing in evangelism is going to turn hearts! Do you know how long that situation would have taken if that man had walked up with a canned approach?

When we witness simply out of our own knowledge and experience, it is far less effective.

> *And he will turn many of the children of Israel to the Lord their God. He will also go before Him in the spirit and power of Elijah, "to turn the hearts of the fathers to the children," and the disobedient to the wisdom of the just, to make ready a people prepared for the Lord* (Luke 1:16-17).

Jesus reveals a new dimension on the Elijah anointing. He says, "The disobedient will turn to the wisdom of the just." The spirit and power of Elijah turns hearts by releasing the most compelling catalyst ever fashioned; it reveals, breaks through, and convinces. The power of this catalyst lies in its ability to convert and convict hearts.

There are no new improvements today of evangelistic techniques that are as effective as flowing with the Elijah anointing. I'm convinced that this dimension was seen in the ministries of Charles Finney, George Whitefield, Maria Woodworth-Etter, and other evangelists. Many testified that their words seemed to penetrate the hearers' very beings. Their words carried more weight and "fastened on" in a way that wasn't easy to shake.

Revivalist Jonathan Edwards preached, and the hearers thought that the ground would open up and hell would swallow them. This anointing alters people's perception of their current situation and current heart condition. It gets released through one's words, expressions, and presence, when an individual is yielded to the Holy Spirit.

Prayer, and spending time soaking in God's presence, is our way of growing in the Elijah anointing. Ultimately, deciding to go forward in God's redemptive purposes is what positions us.

This prophetic mantle of evangelism turns the disobedient to the wisdom of the just. The mantle of this anointing brings conviction.

THE EXPLOITS OF THE ELIJAH ANOINTING:

1. It challenged compromise in the lives of God's people.
2. It called attention to Elijah's message with miracles.
3. It repaired the broken altar of Jehovah.
4. An outpouring came into being, which broke off the drought.
5. Elijah called down fire from Heaven and upstaged the false prophets. As a result, he saw a whole generation turn their hearts back to God.
6. It executed the false prophets after exposing who they were.
7. Elijah was instrumental in seeing the demise of Ahab's entire house.
8. It raised a child from the dead.

NO MORE LIFELESS STAFFS

Elisha had been mentored by Elijah, so let's look at Elisha's servant:

Now Gehazi went on ahead of them, and laid the staff on the face of the child; but there was neither voice nor hearing. Therefore he went back to meet him, and told him, saying, "The child has not awakened." When Elisha came into the house, there was the child, lying dead on his bed. ...And he went up and lay on the child, and put his mouth on his mouth, his eyes on his eyes, and his hands on his hands; and he stretched himself out on the child, and the flesh of the child became warm (2 Kings 4:31-32, 34).

The staff is a lifeless object and represents some of the older programmatic evangelistic tools. This mentality is reflected in the thinking: "Get the lost into the church and we'll get programs for them." But that's the problem; we're not getting the lost to come into the church. We've got to "go into all the world."

MAKE A PARADIGM SHIFT

We've got a generation who's entertained by death. They're attracted by death. They play games about death in video games and in psychic practices.

We've got to be able to speak with words that are meaningful to the world. Not just words that are meaningful to us; not Christian-ese, but what relates to where folks are at. We live in a Christian subculture that we need to bust out of. We've got to see eye to eye to be able to have compassion on the world. There's a whole world outside of our Christian world! We need to see what they see and feel what they feel.

Without the power of the Spirit, accompanied with signs and wonders, we are handicapped in getting a hearing in this generation. They're going to put Christianity up on a shelf with all the other religions and say, "What's the difference?"

When we let compassion and mercy arise in our hearts, something new can happen in us. Something new can flow out of our lives.

A prophetic evangelist can break things wide open. You can be talking to someone who is hardened and God can give you a word for them.

I remember one night, after coming out of a great Christian meeting, we were in a restaurant and I looked at the server. I immediately knew that she was estranged from her mother, her dad was not in the picture, and at this point she was very angry at her mom because she was hurt bitterly. It became totally clear to me.

I didn't want to embarrass her in front of other people, so I followed her away from the table and asked if I could talk to her for a minute. I said, "Hey, you may think this is a little bit out there, but I'm a Christian and I believe God speaks to people, and the Lord spoke to me about you." I laid it out. She was shocked and asked how I knew all of that. I don't know if there could have been anything else that could have brought her to a point where I could have prayed with her besides that prophetic word.

Another time, there was a woman who was also a server, who was all perky when she was taking our order, but the Lord showed me that she had a horrible migraine headache. I had this burden for her, but because she was so excited, I kept pushing it down because it didn't make sense to my mind.

I asked her, "By any chance do you have a headache?" Immediately she said, "Oh, man, I've got the worst headache right now!" I asked her if I could pray for her. She said, "Sure," but she thought I meant sometime later. I said, "No, I mean right now." I took her hand and prayed. She went away and came back kind of subdued saying, "What did you do?" She then told me that her head felt totally fine. I then told her, "Hey, I don't have any power to heal anybody, but God spoke to me about what was wrong, and He just wants you to know that His power is real."

In many instances, I haven't even known beforehand what I was saying. You can read people's mail from A to Z and be unconsciously prophetic.

We need this kind of anointing to break through the wounds of this generation—break through the doubts, break through the people-pleasing, break through the greed. Elisha's experience with the child who was dead is an illustration of prophetic evangelism. With prophetic evangelism, the dead generation rises up.

PIERCING DEFENSES

The prophetic anointing is testifying about the Almighty. When Elijah called down fire it testified about the Almighty. The prophetic anointing on our lives, as it relates to evangelism, is to pierce defenses by manifesting the ultimate testimony. People have a lot of defenses. You are not going to have time in all instances to answer all of the questions, which is why you're going to need the Elijah anointing to turn hearts.

> *Again He said to me, "Prophesy to these bones, and say to them, 'O dry bones, hear the word of the Lord! Thus says the Lord God to these bones: "Surely I will cause breath to enter into you, and you shall live. I will put sinews on you and bring flesh upon you, cover you with skin and put breath in you; and you shall live. Then you shall know that I am the Lord" ' "* (Ezekiel 37:4-6).

Can we all agree that the valley of dry bones is a picture of our generation today? I believe that a prophetic anointing will breathe life into people. We're going to go beyond sharing at a cerebral level, to where God is going to breathe—the Holy Spirit Himself.

We're going to be able to prophesy into the hopeless graveyards of people's hearts. It's going to cause dreams and thoughts to come into their minds. This will make them know they are special and God does have something for them.

A CONFRONTATION WITH THE CONFRONTATIONAL APOLOGIST

I remember a particular time at Chico State when this gentleman came to speak who traveled around to college campuses. He was in his 50s, wore a three-piece suit, and would gather the kids around and start yelling at them. "You brood of vipers, you filthy rotten sinners." He pointed at some sorority girls, and I quote, "A prostitute couldn't make a plug dime on this campus because what they get paid for you're giving up for free." He pointed at a group of guys with long hair and questioned their sexual preferences.

As I was sitting there, getting ready to set up my table, I was distraught. My spirit was screaming within me, "No, no, that's not what Jesus would do!" He continued yelling, "God is going to delight in judging you who have sinned!" (In fact, the Bible says the exact opposite: God does not delight in judging the banished ones, but He devises means whereby the banished ones will be saved—Second Samuel 14:14.)

In the midst of it, I got up and said, "Sir, I disagree with you. I just don't think Jesus would stand up and delight in people going to hell." Earlier he had walked up to me and bragged that he had gone to U.C. Berkeley and told them "like it is." I asked what he meant by that. He told me how he had screamed angrily and judgmentally.

I asked him what happened. He said they had punched him and threw him in a water pond. He was bragging that the fruit of his ministry was that he got beat up. I'm thinking, "The fruit ought to be the presence of God and persecution for righteousness' sake, not persecution for fleshly demonstrations."

So I got up and started preaching Christ by saying, "This guy has shown you exactly what many of you have believed Christianity is about, but that's not what Christianity is about." My heart was actually tender towards them. At the very next meeting, we saw students who had been at that incident who gave their hearts to the Lord.

I felt like the Elijah anointing turned their hearts. Some erroneously think that the Elijah anointing that was on John the Baptist was about yelling and being very hard toward the lost.

John the Baptist was definitely an unusual man. Jesus called him Elijah, for those who could handle it (see Matt. 11:14). He was considered a prophet by the multitudes (see Matt. 14:5) because of the power and influence of his ministry. When John the Baptist spoke, even though he performed no signs, many believed in him, as strange as he appeared to people (see John 10:41-42). The Elijah anointing on John the Baptist was so lethal to darkness that satan went after his head.

In Matthew 11, Jesus asked the multitudes who traveled great distances to see John the Baptist, "What drove you to go there?"

1. "A reed shaken by the wind?" No! Jesus emphasized that the Elijah anointing on John the Baptist delivered him from being a weather vane of human influences. This anointing puts strength in your resolve—no more double-mindedness!

2. "A man clothed in soft garments?" No! This anointing manifests itself in a way where its bearer doesn't look for conveniences, but convictions; there's a grace for self-denial over self-indulgence.

3. "A prophet" Yes! More than a prophet! John the Baptist was not just a prophet, but he was the subject of prophecy. Jesus, in Matthew 11:10, recites Malachi 3:1, and says, "This is he of whom it is written: Behold, I send my messenger before your face, who will prepare your way before you." As we rise up, we will not only be prophetic to our generation, but the subjects of the prophetic, with God's Word foretelling our exploits.

The Welsh Revival

What would it be like if crime stopped in your city? What would it be like if the bars and taverns shut down? What would it be like if the police didn't fight any crime, so they performed Holy Ghost choruses? You may think, "Come on, Sean, be realistic."

The Welsh Revival, 1904: they say it was spiritually dark in Wales and seemed to be getting darker by the day. Bars flourished; there was cock fighting, boxing, gambling, prostitution, and major soccer frenzy (they call it football but Americans call it soccer). All of this seemed to capture the souls of the people. Murder, rape, and other violent crimes were increasing dramatically.

In the midst of all of this, somebody broke out like a plague; a half-educated coal miner by the name of Evan Roberts. He rose up and realized that there was a plague in his area.

There was a young teenaged girl by the name of Florrie Evans. Florrie had recently given her life to the Lord. She stood up in the middle of this small prayer meeting, in the midst of the darkness in that town, and said, "I love Jesus Christ with all me heart."

Now we've all heard that before, but it was as if at that moment, something broke out among the people at that prayer meeting. People who write about the revival say that it began with this young girl. People began sobbing. They felt the need to fall in love with Jesus. People were instantly convicted that they had only been playing church. Maybe they had loved the Lord a little bit, but they hadn't gone all the way with God. Simultaneously, across town, in a coal mine, a guy is coming off his shift coughing up coal dust. He's sweating, and all of a sudden something gripped his heart. The Lord revealed Himself to Evan Roberts in such an amazing and overwhelming manner that he was filled with divine awe and "had a mount of transfiguration," and he would never be the same. Roberts began to witness and became a fire-starter for a move of God.

Practically overnight there came this spiritual revival. Thousands of young converts multiplied across the region, preaching the gospel that had reached them. Newspapers were filled with reports of conversions. They say that there is no other example in history where a region was so quickly and radically transformed into a region of righteousness than in the Welsh Revival. They say the fire of this movement was so intense that when newsletters went out about the revival to other cities, revival would break out there as well.

The men who manned the horses in the mine would normally command them by using curse words and expletives, but they got saved so they weren't cursing anymore. So there was a jam up in the front of the mines because all the oxen and mules knew only curse commands.

The police officers formed barbershop quartets, singing gospel hymns, because there was no more crime. Bars shut down, prostitutes got saved, and soccer players got saved. When the soccer players got saved, they broke out like a plague, and went out onto the streets witnessing. Entire teams were disbanded.

People would go to bars and order drinks, but get under such conviction they wouldn't even be able to drink their drink. They would just walk back out and show up at a church and fall on their faces. Evan Roberts definitely had the Elijah anointing on him!

He often would step into pulpits and weep. This released such a turning heart conviction that hearers would immediately run forward to Christ in tears. Can it happen? Sure it can, if we as believers begin to carry the Elijah anointing. We will be convincing because we are convinced!

CHAPTER 8

THE TONGUE OF THE
LEARNED AND THE AWAKENED EAR

"I'm not ashamed of the gospel...
but I am ashamed of how some Christians communicate it."
—Doug Addison

ONE DAY WE WENT TO THE UNIVERSITY of California at Berkeley for an open-air meeting commemorating the tragedy of 9/11. A guy came up to where I was speaking and manifested a demon right in front of everyone, at the same time I'm trying to speak to a crowd of "spiritually challenged" students.

At that very moment, I had an infusion of wisdom on what to say. I said, "We're here to remember all of the men and women who lost their lives in the terrorists' attack. Thousands have died over the past hundreds of years for your freedom, but only One has died for your soul. And it's not about whether or not you will be remembered by people, but the ultimate thing is whether or not God will remember you. What was important five minutes before the planes hit wasn't important five minutes after they hit; your destiny is important."

There was a quiet moment and I quickly said, "Let's bow our heads." It was awesome! It was the tongue of the learned that happened. All over the crowd, college students bowed their heads.

The Lord God has given me the tongue of the learned, that I should know how to speak a word in season to him who is weary. He awakens Me morning by morning, He awakens My ear to hear as the learned (Isaiah 50:4).

This country desperately needs people who have the tongue of the learned. I'm prophesying to you that you will be given platforms in the days to come! What we need is an awakened ear to hear the battle plans of the Lord.

So often I've prepared a message, but then I'll get in the pulpit and the Lord will direct me another way. Sometimes I find out later that the Lord directed me to change everything for the validation of just one person there. In that moment, I received "the tongue of the learned." God wants to bless us to communicate with sanctified creativity.

Let me define evangelism:

Evangelism is the proclamation and presentation of the gospel of Jesus Christ to persons in the secular age; in such that they will understand its crucial and relevant importance, so that they will respond to Him as Lord and Savior in faith and obedience.

SHIFTING BATTLE LINES

New-school apologetics can be defined as knowing the needs, concerns, and worries of individuals. We can "educate" ourselves by reading the newspaper, watching the news, and listening to conversations at the coffee shop.

Every time evil deepens in society, a new aspect of the gospel rises up. For every problem, the answer is in the gospel. Good apologetics reveal how the Christian gospel is the key—the answer—in the new evils of the world. Folks want to get saved when they understand how the gospel offers them answers.

Old-school apologetics give rational proofs about the death, burial, and resurrection of Jesus Christ, and that Jesus Christ is who He says He is. I'm not saying this is wrong or not being used anymore. I praise God for the apologists who have fought the good fight, but the battle lines have definitely shifted in the last generation.

In Acts 18:4 it says that "he [Paul] **reasoned** in the synagogue... and persuaded."

The definition of "reasoned" (#1256): "mingle thought with thought, revolve in mind, to converse, drawing arguments from Scripture, ponder. The word is translated 'to preach' (in Acts 20:7)."

The definition of "persuade" (#3982): "To have confidence in, convince, seeking the favor, urging, won over; persuaded to a better thing."

These definitions clue us in on prophetic evangelism and words of wisdom.

I'm finding more and more today that as we have turned to an "information-gorged age," the battle lines are much more about experience. People today want to know if what you believe is real—is it relevant. New-school apologetics is shifting. Today, apologetics is about removing the hindrances to someone coming to faith, while setting forth the attractiveness. It's not just setting forth the truths of the gospel; I need to find out prophetically with lost people, "What is the hitch? Why aren't you getting saved?"

FAULT LINES AND WARNING SIGNS

Observing a culture closely allows you to discern its fault lines. People who do not know the Lord have fault lines in their lives, though they may give you the impression that everything is good.

Fault lines are ideas and values in a society that cannot be sustained. They're contradictions. For example, we tell folks, "You are the master of your fate. You're in control. You're a self-made man or woman." On the other side of our mouths we're saying "You're a victim of your circumstances. Your mama ate too many Twinkies when she was pregnant, so you've got Twinkie syndrome."

We've got people trapped in sins, but because they don't feel the power to get free, they want you to change the rules. "Because I can't get free, I want you to change the rules so I can feel justified in the sin I plan on staying in." Being trapped in a lifestyle is a problem Jesus is not intimidated by. We must introduce people to the Genuine One.

Here's what the Gallup Poll said: If you could spend the day with anyone in history, who would it be? Two out of every three Americans (66 percent) chose Jesus as the historical figure that they would most like to spend the day with.

Based on that, why would we think people are turned off to knowing more about Jesus? We need to see a fault line in our generation today. Maybe the fault line is actually in us. The unsaved don't want to come to our churches, but they want to spend time with Jesus. That ought to tell us something! Let's get alone with God and ask Him to adjust the fault line in us.

THE SONS OF ISSACHAR

There was a group of men back in David's time who were small in number, but highly skilled in understanding the times. The men of Issachar were the fewest of all, only 200, yet as valuable to David's army as any others.

From Issachar came "men of understanding" in reference to the times. Their brethren had the fullest confidence in their wisdom, experience, and skill. Nothing was done but by their direction. The sons of Issachar were counter-balanced by their preeminent zeal, shrewdness, and discipline.

These men rose up during a remarkably interesting crisis in the circumstances of the nation. It was a transitional phase where the people's minds and hearts were divided between Saul's house and David's house. We also live in times where philosophies and loyalties are scattered.

The sons of Issachar's characteristics positioned them to be both the best advisors and soldiers in the camp. Their attributes represent the prophetic and the evangelistic streams coming together at a crucial time. They knew political times, understood public affairs, the temper of the nation, and the tendencies of the present events.

The sons of Issachar comprehended the circumstances in which their country was placed; they marked the spirit that prevailed among the people. They analyzed the impulses of their culture and estimated cultural events and their bearing upon society.

The sons of Issachar could look about and see into things, and interpret the forecast written upon a circumstance. Scholars say that the spirit of their age was national indifference and infidelity, just as it is today. Their anointing is needed in our day.

Modern-Day Sons of Issachar:

1. Realize that people have a spiritual hunger and interest. There is an "eternity deficit" in the human heart, which makes people's hearts vulnerable to spirituality—good or bad.

2. Address the cultural touchstones and spokespeople. We must be relevant as well as righteous or we won't have a hearing. A relevant message gains interest as well as addresses things people are familiar with.

3. Interpret the inner yearnings and anguish of the culture. Modern music taps into the pain of a generation, which creates interest and popularity. We are to keep a watchful eye on public affairs, cultural movements, and spiritual currents with a view to discover their bearing on the prospects of the Body of Christ.

4. Fully utilize your *pathos* arrows. Nothing is more heartfelt than Christ's story. We will see hearts captivated as we attend to the inner passions of our hearers. *Pathos* refers to the emotional aspects of appeals to the heart.

5. Take advantage of "tipping points" and "trigger" moments. These moments are times when people are ready to change; when circumstances and conscience dictate openness to the eternal wisdom of God.

Becoming students of our culture allows us to release a prophetic embodiment of what the Spirit of God is breathing through our gospel. Missiologists call this contextualization. We need to understand the signs and seasons of our times.

Supernatural Download

Our job today is to bring out the attraction of the gospel by grounding it in the situation of the people we talk to. That's why a generic approach to sharing the gospel will not be as effective as having "an awakened ear" to hear the hearts of people. Don't just hear what they're saying; *hear what they're saying.*

There are a lot of folks who hide behind statements that are smoke screens, but you have to listen for the voice of their heart. As you have an awakened ear, you'll be able to hear what's going on in a person's life, and you'll be able to have the tongue of the learned. You'll be able to speak into people's situations. This is often in the form of a word of wisdom.

A word of wisdom is a spontaneous revelation of wise guidance or knowledge rightly applied.

> *Therefore settle it in your hearts not to meditate beforehand on what you will answer; for I will give you a mouth and wisdom which all your adversaries will not be able to contradict or resist* (Luke 21:14-15).

You're going to be brought into situations where thinking through and rehearsing what you should say will not be the key. Jesus will supernaturally download wisdom to give you insight into what a person is going through.

What God wants to give us is the ability to articulate the mystery of what is going on in a person's heart—that empty place. We are to connect that empty place with the love of Jesus Christ. I cannot go out trusting my own intelligence and wit, but I can go out having faith that God will cause evangelism to become prophetic. It's a supernatural download!

CUTTING THROUGH THE FOG

Once there was a man who did this intellectual debating presentation at San Francisco State University. He came out and intellectually pounded people with his deep theological knowledge. He would use secular arguments and reasoning and get them to agree on a premise and then destroy the premise out from underneath them. They would then cave and fall in. This is a strategy of modern debate. The gay and lesbian student alliance club was there, and they literally picked this guy up with his placards and threw him and his stuff off campus.

I came the following week. I didn't even know what I was going to share. I was so nervous wondering if they were going to throw me out and beat me up, too. I shared about what it was like growing up without a dad, and the sting of fatherlessness, which I call an orphan spirit.

I didn't know until much later, that one of the major wounds (not for all but for many) of people who are trapped in the confusion of their sexual identity is that many of them have had a bad experience with their father. I just shared with them my life and testimony and guess what happened? Five of them walked forward, breaking through the crowd on the San Francisco State campus, and gave their lives to Jesus Christ. One week earlier, the man who could intellectually run circles around me had been thrown off campus by these same students.

LOST IN TRANSLATION

Missionaries have been expected to learn the language of the people they have been called to reach. Daniel the prophet, who was abruptly dropped off in Babylon, consented to learn the language and culture of Babylon. He refused to drink the wine of the culture, demonstrating the balance needed to be a reformer. Daniel spoke the language of Babylon, but didn't sip of the spirit (or wine) of Babylon. Having a command of the culture and sensitivity to the new wine (the Holy Spirit) allows one to interpret the dreams of the culture.

Reformer Peter Waldo sponsored translators of the Bible in local languages. The Waldenses stressed the importance of preaching, and they allowed both laymen and laywomen to preach. They preached to people in the local language. Refusing to use the Latin, they made the gospel clearly understandable to all.

The major difference between reformers and refugees is their ability to decode and deliver their culture. A refugee is a displaced exile, forced to flee what is home for them. A reformer contends to bring about correction for abuses and justice, right where they live.

Daniel demonstrates for us how to acquire the tongue of the learned (see Dan. 5:11-14). He was known for waiting on the Lord to get the strategy of God for a situation. When Daniel was able to interpret dreams, they said "this man has the insights of the gods in him." That's the wisdom that God wants to give us: intelligence that is evidenced in discovering the meaning of mysteries.

The word *wisdom* means knowledge of diverse matters. God says that "when I give you wisdom, I'm going to give you knowledge of diverse matters." It is the mysteries of people's hearts that we need to interpret.

AN AWAKENED EAR

We must have a "now" word to speak to this generation. An awakened ear leads to a "now" word that can release an awakening. We can't speak today as we did yesterday or our witness will fall on deaf ears. Society has changed.

The tongue of the learned allows you to break through the static of the culture. It allows you to speak from a fresh perspective and engage the hearer.

We, like Daniel, must give meaning to the secrets of people's hearts. We must be the ones who make sense of life amidst cultural ambiguities.

Wisdom also means proper prudence in interacting with the lost. Claim wisdom as yours! "Lord, You said You'd give me wisdom. You said You'd give me knowledge of diverse matters. I'm going to study. I'm going to show myself approved, but I'm going to believe for that moment of supernatural download. I'm going to believe for intelligence and evidence in discerning the mysteries of men and women's hearts in our culture and in our society."

EMPHATIC AND SOCRATIC

There was an early Greek philosopher, Socrates, who was credited for utilizing a method of persuasion that employed challenging the assumptions of people by asking probing questions. He could keep the conversation under his direction while undermining the "fault lines" of others' logic. A good question becomes a prophetic smart bomb that passes the defenses of objectors, without cramming our ideas down their throats.

There are questions that cause someone to take a different look at what they are thinking. There are questions that call upon someone to explain and defend their reasoning. Jesus had the ability to turn objections into opportunities.

Francis Schaeffer, the great Christian thinker, once said, "No one can live logically according to his own non-Christian presuppositions." He was hitting on the fact that any other worldview will have "fault lines," and will reveal inconsistencies.

There was an argumentation class offered at my college that covered instruction on special methods of refutation, which included "turning the tables." This involved asking questions that revealed contrary conclusions, prompting the self-questioning of one's philosophy.

If you are witnessing to a person who believes in evolution, causing them to view their beliefs through the lens of practicality would reveal difficulties in plausibility. You could ask them if they would believe that a hurricane passing through a junkyard could produce a Boeing jet. To believe that a lightning bolt could produce the complexity of human life is actually less likely than the "accidental" jet.

We want non-Christians to check the finished product of their philosophy. This method, when breathed upon by the Spirit, is effective, as it helps you to focus upon winning their souls versus winning the argument.

Psychologist Carole Lieberman has said, "When a distraction evaporates, you have to come face to face with your own troubles." Their beliefs are wrong because the presuppositions they take for granted are wrong.

Many times I can remember seeing a physician when I was young, and I always felt nervous. The doctor would check my ears, throat, and heart. Based upon the "bug" I had, the doctor would give me a prescription. A prescription is not some vague, over-the-counter, generic cure-all, but a unique antidote, especially fashioned for a specific problem. In this age we need divine prescriptions to counteract the dark viruses of unbelief prevalent in our generation. It's vital that beyond knowing the problem, we have an especially fashioned wisdom for knowing how to conquer the problem.

When we become open to the Holy Spirit, implanting within us the Spirit of counsel, we have divine prescriptions rather than human precepts.

MOUTH-TO-MOUTH RESUSCITATION

When Elisha came into the house, there was the child, lying dead on his bed. He went in therefore, shut the door behind the two of them, and prayed to the Lord. And he went up and lay on the child, and put his mouth on his mouth, his eyes on his eyes, and his hands on his hands; and he stretched himself out on the child, and the flesh of the child became warm (2 Kings 4:32-34).

I can relate to Elisha's ministry a little bit. This guy did something and initially it didn't seem to be the Lord's plan, but he didn't quit. He didn't get discouraged. No, he learned something.

I believe that we've had an impersonal, non-relational approach, and it's not working. I'm not saying you shouldn't use tracts. But I am saying that there are more tools to use. Today, we have to relate to where folks are in their lives. Mouth-to-mouth illustrates the value of having the tongue of the learned. What Elisha did physically, we must do spiritually, by connecting to their hearts.

Continuing with Elisha's story, laying the staff on the child did not revive him. So Elisha went in and closed the door. We need to remove as many distractions as possible in our lives and begin to focus on how to get an understanding of where lost people are.

THE IDENTIFICATION FACTOR

The more closely you identify with your hearers, the more it's going to help the weight of your words. The ability to verbalize the gospel in words they can clearly understand is key. Practice by writing down what the gospel is in a paragraph. I want to challenge you. Every day, think of a fresh, redemptive way to phrase the gospel. Talk to people and find out what's going on in their lives right now so you can think of new ways to relate to them.

Rather than speak in Christian terms that the unchurched don't understand, find the dynamic equivalent. How can I say "washed in the blood" in a different way? Ask yourself where you're saying words that don't mean anything to the world. We must make sure that we are communicating in ways that people can understand. Revivalist Charles Finney said, "God's revelation to people does not usually suspend laws of the human mind and human audience, but occurs through those laws."

Church father, Augustine, recommended that the Christian minister "plunder the Egyptians for their gold," implying that we should learn secular communication to better communicate our gospel. God is a God of creativity. Can't He give you a strategy and approach that is fresh and anointed?

THREE FACTORS THAT INFLUENCE PEOPLE

1. *Logos* **(reason).** There are excellent, rational statements to say to unsaved people. For example, sin leaves a wound. When you relate to their hurting, you can give Something (Someone) people need.

2. *Pathos* **(emotions).** Appeal to the heart. You were never intended by God to live in the pain you're living in right now.

3. *Ethos* **(experience).** Relationship helps because you know what a person is going through. For example, after tragedies, people are open to prayer. We're going to be surprised to see who's in Heaven because there are so many deathbed salvations.

KERYGMA—PUBLIC PROCLAMATION

It's interesting that on the day of Pentecost, God chose the emblem of the flaming tongue to signify the launching of the Church. From that point on the tongues of the early believers were catalysts for revival and phenomenal harvest.

Biblical scholars have focused on the New Testament concepts of *kerygma* and *didaskein*. Didaskein is defined as teaching that centers on the doctrine, while kerygma is the public declaration of the gospel to the lost world with the purpose of conversions. In First Corinthians 1:21, Paul uses kerygma when he says, "It pleased God through the foolishness of the message preached to save those who believe." We must recapture the power of kerygma in today's context. I am convinced that there is an anointing to preach which causes the words of the believer to be launched into the hearts of the people.

SPEECH IMPEDIMENT

Then Moses said to the Lord, "O my Lord, I am not eloquent, neither before nor since You have spoken to Your servant; but I am slow of speech and slow of tongue." So the Lord said to him, "Who has made man's mouth? Or who makes the mute, the deaf, the seeing, or the blind? Have not I, the Lord?" (Exodus 4:10-11)

God possesses unlimited power over all of man's senses. He could impart to Moses the giftings necessary to get the job done. He gives the quintessential catchphrases. The term "slow tongue," in verse 10, implies a difficulty in finding words, and in giving them utterance.

THE USELESSNESS OF MERE WORDS

There's always the feeling that you could speak better than you do. Moses didn't feel he was gifted with persuasion. To date, the patriarch Moses holds the record for the greatest altar response ever. He saw several million come out of darkness into light in one miraculous moment. Today's prophetic evangelists are faced with an equally monumental undertaking. World population statistics affirm that barring a divine intervention that results in massive harvest, more people stand to go to hell in this generation than all the previous generations combined. Moses represents an Old Testament type of a new breed of New Testament prophetic evangelist.

In Exodus 4, Moses questioned whether Pharaoh, Egypt, and the captive Israelites would listen to his voice. The Hebrew word for "voice" is also the word for "sound." There's a desperate need for the Body of Christ to have the right sound for this postmodern age. There's a sound from Heaven that we must tap into.

The only way to achieve this is by God teaching us what to say. The great Christian author, J.B. Phillips, said, "If words are to enter people's hearts and bear fruit, they must be the right words shaped to pass defenses and explode silently and effectually within their minds." We need a new sound—words that hit home, words that achieve deliverance of hearts and attract people to come under the sound of the gospel.

This electrifying truth underscores the fact that our "sound" must negotiate its way past cerebral armor in order to captivate hearts. This is the gift of the tongue of the learned, which cuts into the souls of the listeners. We need these "arrows of the Lord."

Moses realized the truth that our ideas are dependent on our language. He also recognized that language used poorly can damage your message and forge an argument against you. The power of speech can never be underestimated. God created us in His image, and God is absolutely a communicator. He dropped His DNA in His children to vocalize and verbalize. Jesus declared that He was sent "to proclaim freedom for captives." Many who witness miracles in the making, hit snags because Christians struggle to find the right words.

Our modern media is filled with "talking heads" and what we really need is "talking hearts." If we come from our hearts, God will allow us to tune into His mind. Since we've been given the mind of Christ, the most important thing is to tune into love and righteousness. It is then that God releases the tongue of the learned. Our confidence comes from our dependence. We cannot have the Book of Acts results without going public with the gospel.

The values and visions of culture are crafted by the speech of its "preachers."

Moses tried to excuse himself for not being eloquent. God told Moses that He would be with his mouth and teach him what to say (see Exod. 4:12). When God teaches your mouth, you have what Isaiah referred to as the "tongue of the learned." An eloquent voice is quite different from carelessly throwing around lofty words. An eloquent voice is essentially a God-given gift that turns an ordinary talker into a spellbinding communicator. This theme is crucial as to how we interact in a cultural paradigm that is unreceptive to our faith.

When Moses told the Lord that he was not eloquent, he was in essence saying that he didn't feel like he would have a significant bearing on the matter before him. What Moses needed, in addition to spiritual leverage, was relevance. The Latin root word for *relevance* simply means, "to bear upon." Author Terry Crist says, "Spiritual relevance is the act of communicating truth in such a way that it has personal bearing on its recipients."

God's solution for slow tongues is bringing about a fast track of fresh dependence in His mouthpieces. When you feel tongue-tied, God wants you to know that He can loose it and set it on fire. The Bible promises that He will make you a fisher of men and teach you what to say—all we have to do is stay yielded to His promptings.

WHAT DOES IT MEAN TO HAVE
GOD BE WITH YOUR MOUTH?

1. You speak words that release vitality.
2. You come with a fresh perspective.
3. You communicate reality.
4. Your words fasten themselves in listeners' souls.
5. You vocalize the mysteries that resonate with the hearts of the hearers.

I will be with your mouth and teach you what you shall say (Exodus 4:12).

The Hebrew word for *teach* means: (1) To flow as water, (2) to shoot as an arrow, and (3) to point out by aiming the finger.

These three shades of meanings give us clues for how to acquire the tongue of the learned:

1. To "flow as water" tells us that we must get in the current of God's movement. We do this by developing sensitivity to God's Spirit through devotion. Flowing as water means that it's not a series of stopping and going, but being fluent as an oracle of God. God wants you to sense His peace while easily articulating His words to others.

2. To "shoot as an arrow" reflects the need to have precise words that accurately hit their target. Our target is not intellectual stimulation, but heart conversion. Arrows were serious weaponry to the ancients. Arrows speak of the fact that there is something we should aim for.

We want to be engaging; we want to move people to action. The tongue of the learned then becomes a launching pad for the artillery of the anointed. Impact begins when we realize that we are agents of influence.

3. Finally, the Lord will use His finger to point out a strategy that when the truth is spoken, an outcome is affected. He will point out vulnerability, heartache, inner desire and destinies, if we will listen. These will become "openings" of the gospel when shared with love.

The great orator, C.H. Spurgeon, said, "The best attraction is the gospel in its purity." Know your audience. Be a person who has an awakened ear and the tongue of the learned.

154

How to Have the Tongue of the Learned

Here are some principles of effective gospel communicators:

1. Relate to people out of positive assumptions, not negative assumptions. Good salesmen assume you want to buy their product. Believe that the person before you wants to be free, and needs the light you possess.

2. Engage people on secular mutual ground. Meet folks on their turf, their classroom, their car, their favorite restaurant. Don't wait until people come into church.

3. Be an active listener. Listening is like currency. Let people share their heart and they will let you share yours.

4. Speak to the questions, unmet needs, and unfulfilled moments that drive people's lives. Speak to the area in their lives that is their need. A lot of secular people have a false assumption that the gospel is not relevant. But when you share how the Good News will meet their need, it immediately leaps off the antiquated pages in their mind and into the relevant impact of where they're living right now.

5. Fully utilize storytelling, metaphors, and redemptive analogies. The ability to turn a metaphor is a key to communicating to this generation. Stories are always less threatening and more effective in illustrating truth.

Action Step Addendum
Tapping Into God's Frequency

Acts 2:17 says, "It shall come to pass in the last days...that I will pour out My Spirit on all flesh; your sons and daughters shall prophesy...." I'm convinced that in this century the revelatory gifts will experience a definite and dramatic increase in both frequency and intensity. In light of this, Christians need to develop their revelation receivers. Elijah said, "Lord...I have done all these things at Your word" (see 1 Kings 18:36). This is the secret to miracles and moving hearts.

Tips for Tapping Into God's Frequency

1. Know that God is a communicator (see Ps. 139:17-18). God is constantly transmitting His thoughts to us (see Ps. 40:5).

2. The prophetic is available to you (see 1 Cor. 14:24,31). God has equipped you to minister in the prophetic. The Holy Spirit dwells inside of you and He is the Spirit of counsel and might. Discernment comes as a process of growth.

3. Recognize God's voice (see John 10:27).

   a. God's voice is consistent with His nature, so you must know His Word.

   b. God's voice comes to you like "a sudden awareness, associated with a unique conviction." It interrupts your thought patterns.

   c. God's voice has unusual content to it—His words are profoundly more loving, wiser, and purer than human thought.

   d. God's voice can come as impressions, pictures, burdens, and spiritual sensing.

   e. God's leading can manifest as being drawn to someone.

   f. God's voice has characteristics of peace, brings clarity, deep conviction, stays with you, and is focused on others.

4. Become still to tune into God's activity (see Ps. 46:10). Spend time meditating on God's promises. We have to look away from everything else in order to see the supernatural. As we wait for His counsel, the increase of revelation will come.

5. Acclimate your environment (see Ps. 22:3). If His presence doesn't dominate where you are, something else will. Pray and worship in the Spirit. Praise acts as a spiritual broom to sweep the mind.

6. Recognize and respect the person of the Holy Spirit (see 2 Cor. 13:14). Fellowship with Him and give Him place. We must learn to treasure the Holy Spirit more than His manifestations. Talk to the Holy Spirit and find out what pleases Him.

7. Live with expectation (see Hab. 2:1). Develop the discipline of awareness and availability. Keep stepping out in faith and you will become more sensitive to His presence and voice (see Heb. 5:14). You must find your flow—how God's Spirit leads you.

   a. Pray and desire spiritual gifts (see 1 Cor. 14:1).

   b. Ask the Holy Spirit to sanctify your imagination.

We need the Holy Spirit to purify our thoughts and calm the troubled waters of our souls. As we submit our thought life to the Holy Spirit, He will release His thoughts to us.

CHAPTER 9

MANIFEST THE MYSTERY

ALL OF HUMANITY WAS CREATED BY GOD to both touch and be touched by the mystery of God. You have been created to be touched by that which is trans-rational. In fact there is an irrepressible spirituality within human nature that cannot be denied; it's a mystery. *Mystery* defined in the Greek means "to shut the mouth, a hidden thing. A mystic or hidden sense; not obvious to the understanding."

God wants to manifest His presence in signs and wonders in a way that will make skeptics gasp. The questions and debates cease when they see the mystery of God.

There are things that are now hidden, that in the endtimes will be revealed by the Lord. I believe He's waiting for such a time and a generation as this to reveal His mysteries. It's by our spirits that we know the things of God. It's the spirit of a man that knows the things of the Spirit.

We have tried to make our gospel political and palatable. But in the midst of this, we've watered down the gospel; we've taken the mystery out of it. Intervarsity author Rick Richardson says, "Mystery is very attractive to people today. People want an experience more than an explanation." We've thought that a generation wants answers, but I submit to you that what they really need in this hour are mysteries.

We have a generation who is raised on supernatural-centered TV shows and books; this generation is not looking for the same ol', same ol' religiosity. They don't want the normal—they want something beyond.

159

This is good, because the spirits of men and women are meant to feed on the mystery of God.

The word *manifest* means to make visible or known that which has been unknown or hidden, whether by words, deeds, or any other way.

Now put it all together. To manifest the mystery is to make known what has been unknown and hidden, whether by words or deeds, that which will shut the mouth. A mystery is a hidden thing; it denotes the hidden sense, and it's not obvious to the understanding.

This is exactly what God is calling us to. There is such an attempt to normalize Christianity, to make it so normal that everyone can understand it. But God's ways are past finding out. "His ways are above our ways; His thoughts are above our thoughts." There are aspects of God I still won't fathom, even in eons of eternity. Any God that we can totally understand becomes something less than God; it becomes a figment of our imagination.

We can love God on the basis of His nature, but we tend not to embrace the aspect of His nature that is mysterious. We miss what God is really all about. There's going to be a challenge for us to stand in faith with that which is mysterious with God. God is tender, but He's tough. He's a God who is just, but He's a God of mercy. Our minds can't wrap around that. We think it's got to be either one or the other.

God wants your faith to be experientially based on more than what you can figure out. Paul said, "Our gospel didn't come to you with wise and persuasive words but with the demonstration of the Holy Ghost and power" (1 Cor. 2:4-5). Biblical faith rests upon the power of God.

You were born from above to walk in this mystery, and the sooner you embrace it, the sooner you'll be able to manifest it to the world.

And He said to them, "To you it has been given to know the mystery of the kingdom of God; but to those who are outside, all things come in parables..." (Mark 4:11).

God wants you to know the mystery. What I mean by mystery is that by our own human ability we cannot figure it out. But God can give us a revelation of the mystery. You and I are supposed to know the mystery because if we know it, we can be conduits for His power and influence.

Let a man so consider us, as servants of Christ and stewards of the mysteries of God (1 Corinthians 4:1).

We have to embrace the mystery before we can manifest the mystery. We must be regarded by humanity as traffickers of servanthood and stewards of the mysteries of God.

I remember one time I was ministering at an altar and a young man came up looking a little puzzled. He just seemed intellectually bound. He said to me, "Would you pray for me, because my mind won't let my heart go free." That's exactly the box that God wants to break us out of. So often our mind, in its desire to understand, won't let our heart feed on the mystery of God.

We all get sucked into a good mystery from time to time. Mysteries begin with a "felt discrepancy," as the experts would call it. I'll call it an itch born of ambiguity, a thing you don't quite understand. These mysteries interrupt something in the beginning to show you a piece of something, but not the whole piece, so you don't feel like you have closure. You're then sucked into watching or reading this mystery so you can have closure and go to bed peacefully.

THE LORD WORKS IN MYSTERIOUS WAYS

If you were to cast your vote for the most often mistaken phrase that people think is in the Bible, what would it be? "The Lord works in mysterious ways." People will quote that and say, "You know what the Bible says, 'The Lord works in mysterious ways.' " No, it's not a verse in the Bible, but it's in the Bible.

"For My thoughts are not your thoughts, nor are your ways My ways," says the Lord. "For as the heavens are higher than the earth, so are My ways higher than your ways, and My thoughts than your thoughts" (Isaiah 55:8-9).

There's a dimension of His ways and thoughts that we do not understand. Although the mysterious God phrase is not in the Bible, this statement may contain more truth than many theologians would care to admit. God is transcendent; He's beyond figuring out; He's beyond our calculations. Many times we are focused on what is naturally sensed,

161

and we try to confine reality to what is rational or tangible. But this ignores the reality of the spiritual universe.

Nothing should be discounted as unbiblical because it seems strange to us. If we start to discount that which we find strange as being unbiblical, we soon find out that we wouldn't have very many pages left in the Bible. If I were to define "manifest the mystery," I would say God wants to jump out of the boxes we put Him in. Reason begins by recognizing what it can never know. Seventeenth-century mathematician Blaise Pascal says, "Reason cannot decide anything." He goes on to articulate that submission is the correct use of reason.

All of a sudden your mind is drawn to a friend of yours, but you don't know why. You might dismiss it and look for natural causes. We always want to connect things with natural reasons, but maybe the mystery is being made manifest and God may be using you for some purpose.

If you don't understand the importance of mystery, you will be limited in being a prophetic evangelist because things will always have to make sense to you. Maybe God would have you do a prophetic act, and in your own mind you're thinking, "There's no connection with me doing this little thing." But God releases something so powerful in your obedience.

There are three Hebrew words for signs and wonders:

1. *Oth* (see Exod. 4:8-9)—This word for signs and wonders refers to something that points beyond itself. It's those events that grab people's attention and points them to God's presence. God will give you mysteries that will grab your attention and point you toward Him.

2. *Pele*—To do something extraordinary, something not explainable by natural cause. This word for signs and wonders could easily be defined as mystery. Something that grabs people's attention and points them to God's presence is beyond itself.

3. *Mophet*—It combines both the idea of the miracle and that of a sign. Scholars say, "It emphasizes that the supernatural event has meaning and significance." So even though it may come as a mystery, it may have significance and meaning to people.

When you manifest the mystery, you are saying, "I've fed on mysteries, so this is not foreign to me. I'm willing to step out and do those

162

things that God tells me to do." Can you imagine when the Holy Spirit said to Jesus, "Spit in the dirt, make it into mud, and put it in the guy's eye and then tell him to go wash"? The man is blind and he now has mud in his eyes! Somehow he gets to the pool and washes and now he can see! We would have said, "Well, that doesn't make sense; God would never tell me to do that." We all know it was worth it when the man washed and was suddenly able to see! In the Book of Acts, in the pre-scientific age, they recognized spiritual realities. For example, angels could bust you out of prison. They believed that they could speak to a guy who had been lame and he could get up and walk. They just believed and miracles happened! Today we stop at the point of struggle and we don't see more miracles, because we don't release God when we can't understand something. There is a transition from human knowledge to knowing God and experiencing His realm.

Jesus held a little child one day and said, "Unless you become as one of these, you cannot even see the kingdom of God." I believe we won't see the dimension of power or the unexplainable dimensions, unless we become like a little child.

There's a shifting taking place in the Western world. Answers will not do when an unveiling is needed. I believe the Western world is now a lot more open to the spirit realm than ever before.

Our problems have outpaced science and technology and we are in need of some unique answers that materialism and rationalism have not been able to give us.

MYSTERY DEPRIVATION

When our brand of Christianity has a mystery deprivation, the occult always picks up the pieces. Satan dines on those areas we have left untouched. We are people who lay down thousands of dollars every day to listen to psychics, who are doing record business. People are desperate to hear something beyond themselves, and if we (who are saved) have a mystery deprivation, that's where the world goes. They will turn to the occult to satisfy their hunger for mystery.

During the Age of Enlightenment, there were great thinkers. These great thinkers felt that Christianity got a little too spiritual. Christianity

163

asked them to agree with realities they weren't ready to leap with because they were limited to just feeding from the tree of good and evil (intellectual knowledge). They weren't ready to feed from the tree of life (the mystery).

As a result, Gnosticism began to creep into the Church and it became very religious, and very predictable. Scholars tell us that it was during that time that paganism was launched into mainstream society. All those thinkers had "de-mystified" Christianity, so society converted to paganism, which is the modern-day occult. Early paganism is the root of the modern occult. Everything from little witches flying on brooms, to cartoons that are doing supernatural acts. This is just history repeating itself, folks!

Back when supernatural signs and wonders and the mystery of God were shown the back door of the church, people thought that materialism might be the answer, or that rationalism could save them. That was the birth of the modern-day witchcraft movement. This is what Isaiah 8:18-19 is saying, "If we're not experiencing these signs and wonders, we will seek those who are mediums and witches." If you do not taste of the mystery of God, then you will be susceptible to the mystery of iniquity. Satan has the right to counterfeit anything that we, by default, don't walk in and use. When we drop the ball on that which we don't understand, the enemy will pick up that mystery, make it marketable, and have people get all over it. Prophetic minister Rick Joyner has said, "The day of supernatural neutrality is over. The lines of demarcation are being drawn."

I believe that he's prophesying. I believe there will be people who are walking radically in the power of God, and people who will be walking radically in the power of darkness, and the day of supernatural neutrality will be over. We're going to have to make a choice, one way or the other. If we have not embraced the mystery of God, we will be increasingly seduced into the mystery of iniquity (see 2 Thess. 2:7).

ARRESTED ATTENTION

In Exodus 3, the Israelites need deliverance. Moses is the soon-to-be-deliverer, but for now he's working for his father-in-law, with sheep, on the backside of the desert. The problem is, the deliverer needs deliverance. How does God manifest Himself to Moses? Moses is walking along in the desert minding his own business. All of a sudden, there's this bush, and it's on fire! God manifested Himself as a mystery to Moses. When Moses saw the bush he said, "I will turn aside to see this great sight and why this bush is burning."

Believers ought to be a burning bush to our world. Folks should be saying, "I've got to turn aside and see the great sight that goes on in that church. There's a mystery going on in there!"

Our lives ought to manifest the mystery. What was the burning bush? It was a picture of what Moses was going to be, as well as what the nation of Israel would be before Pharaoh. It was as if they said to Pharaoh, "Despite all the destructive stuff that you do, we're going to manifest the mystery and thrive in this antagonistic environment. I'm not going to burn up, because God is on me."

The purpose of the bush was to arrest the attention and awaken the consciousness of Moses, realizing that this was something out of the ordinary. Here is the bush—the physical, material, and natural—but in it and on it (the fire) is the immaterial, the spiritual, and the metaphysical. God is putting some "fuel-less" fire on today's prophetic evangelists.

The burning bush was a model. It's a model of what our Christianity ought to look like. Our Christianity ought to manifest the miracle and not be ashamed, recognizing that when people see the miracles, they're going to know that it's God.

The bush was a mystery. It was a model of what was to come, but it was a mystery, a miracle. Moses knew that if God could keep the bush alive, God could preserve him when he was sent to Pharaoh. He knew that he would have to walk in and speak with Pharaoh, who was the strongest military tyrant of that day. Egypt had held a group of people in captivity for four centuries and Moses was just going to walk up to Pharaoh and say, "Hey man, by the way, let the people go"?

If God can manifest the mystery in a bush, God can manifest the mystery in us, even if we can't always figure things out. The first step of a mystery is to upset the equilibrium of the observer.

Scholars say that the bush was a thorny shrub bush that could be found anywhere in the desert. But this bush was special because it had a fuel-less fire on it. God says, "I'm going to put a fuel-less fire on you and it will attract the attention of a lost nation."

The bush was like a magnet that draws. I believe that God is putting on people an "attraction gift." We don't realize it but people are drawn to us. Here was a fire on a plain thorny bush that you could find anywhere in the desert. Just like that plain old bush, when there is a touch of God on your life, people are drawn like a magnet to you.

One of the weaknesses of many of our evangelistic efforts is our lack of the supernatural. I believe we will lose a generation if our only approach in evangelism is either intellectual arguments or emotional appeals. We've got to manifest the miracle of God.

We've got to see the power of God manifested in our midst. Saint Augustine said, "I would never have been a Christian but for miracles." There is a push today to program the Christian experience in such a way that everyone is comfortable with everything that goes on in church. The challenge is this: Whose comfort level should we meet? Do we aim at the folks who have seen the power of God? Or do we aim at the person walking in off the street who doesn't know anything about God?

Unfortunately, what I am seeing in some churches that have experienced the power of the Holy Ghost is that they're aiming at the comfort level of the person who would be uncomfortable with anything showing up! We cannot aim for the lowest common denominator and their comfort level.

I submit to you, we shouldn't even aim for the comfort level of the person who has experienced the power of God before. We ought to aim for everything that God would spill over the edges of Heaven and pour into our services—manifestations beyond what anyone has ever experienced, beyond what any of us has ever tasted.

I need God! My world needs God! I believe that evangelism is a supernatural process and it's never about being clever; it's about manifesting the mystery. It's the fire of God on us.

IF IT WORKS ON YOU, IT SHOULD WORK ON THEM

Then Moses answered and said, "But suppose they will not believe me or listen to my voice; suppose they say, 'The Lord has not appeared to you' " (Exodus 4:1).

God got Moses' attention with a mystery. The way that God got Moses' attention was the same way that God wanted to disrupt dark powers, by manifesting the mystery. Moses' rod was a manifesting of the mystery rod. Moses threw it on the ground; it became a snake. He touched water with it; the water became blood. He pointed it at a sea and it parted; he pointed it at the ground, and dust turned to lice. It is a mystery stick.

Today God is saying, "The same thing that I secured you with (a mystery), is the same thing that you're going to use to get folks free." Manifesting the mystery is about a blatant disruption of the demonic realm. Mysteries are going to pose a new threat to darkness. I believe that this generation is not looking for the palatable; they're looking for the paranormal, that which is off the chart.

Here's what we need more than anything else. When Moses presents himself before Pharaoh, Jannes and Jambres are also there, manifesting their mystery of darkness. Those who present the greatest mystery are going to hold the greatest influence.

Then the magicians of Egypt did so with their enchantments; and Pharaoh's heart grew hard, and he did not heed them, as the Lord had said (Exodus 7:22).

When Moses manifested his mystery and then the magicians (Jannes and Jambres) performed theirs as well, Pharaoh didn't budge; he wasn't convinced. Moses did what they could also do.

Now the magicians so worked with their enchantments to bring forth lice, but they could not. So there were lice on man and beast (Exodus 8:18).

Finally, they couldn't duplicate it and had to admit that it was truly "the finger of God." They could manipulate frogs coming out, they could do a water and blood trick, they could do a little stick to snake trick, but this was a creative miracle. He turned dust into lice. Satan doesn't have anything that's creative. All his powers are destructive, but God's given us the prophetic that is creative.

Prophetic minister, Kris Vallotton, is correct in saying, "I believe that Pharaoh is about to let go of our cities as God demonstrates His raw power through His Church. Yet, there remains a distance between what should be and what will be." We need an extreme revolution in our understanding of the spirit realm, an extreme shift of how ministry takes place. That's what God did to Moses. It began with a burning bush, and it ended with a stick in a man's hand that he lifted up and an ocean of water parted, and an entire nation went free. But it began with God being God.

Manifesting the mystery says this, "I can forge ahead, in faith, without knowing exactly how it's going to turn out. I can forge ahead without even understanding all of the things that are involved, because I have tasted the mystery of God and I can trust Him enough to be in a place where I don't have all of the answers."

THE ORIGINAL IMAX EXPERIENCE

Now all the people witnessed the thunderings, the lightning flashes, the sound of the trumpet, and the mountain smoking; and when the people saw it, they trembled and stood afar off (Exodus 20:18).

Here is God up on the mountain. There's smoke, thunder, sounds of trumpets, and lightning. This is when God introduces Himself to the nation of Israel. He didn't hand them a sheet of facts about who He was. He didn't hand them a set of propositional truths, and then give them an experience with Himself later on in their walk. Israel had the exact opposite. God said, "Experience Me, and then we'll talk."

This is the opposite of the way we do it. We think that we have to talk and prep people for a possible experience that they may or may not have with God. I'm not saying that this is always wrong, but this isn't the way that God revealed Himself to His people here.

It's going to take some level of aggressiveness for us to enter into the unexplainable dimensions of God. It's not just going to drop into our laps; we're going to have to press in.

The tragedy will be if there are unexplainable dimensions that we don't come into because: (a) We feel that if we can't explain it then it must not be legitimate or valid, or (b) we don't recognize that we have to press in to enter into those areas.

What was the purpose of God introducing Himself like that to the Israelites? God was revealing Himself as "One which is altogether other." Jesus is our Friend and our Brother and we need to approach the throne of grace with boldness. But there is going to come a time when we need to recognize that He is altogether other than us.

The other thing that God was doing was curing them from ever trivializing God and His abilities. Once you're introduced to a God who has an IMAX Dolby surround sound event up on a mountain, and later on He tells you He's going to get you into the Promised Land, you can easily believe for Him to move. You don't doubt once you've seen and embraced the mystery of God.

If God were presented to you as someone understandable, when you got into a situation where you could not understand it, you would be stuck. If we're not being fed on the mystery of God, it will be a mystery as to how we're going to get through tough situations. We must have a revelation of the mystery before we can have a manifestation of the mystery.

Our church services are more of a reflection of our nature than that of God's nature.

I believe that this place of revelation is where our churches need to come. It's as if we're saying, like the Israelites did, "Moses, you speak to us and give us what man can give us; we're comfortable with that. But if God shows up in His mystery and awe, we're going to back away."

Now God told them the reason why He presented Himself like He did. He said, "I did it to test you. To see if you would have the fear of God in your heart." In other words, "I want you to have the awe of who I am in your heart." I believe that sometimes God manifests the mystery to test our hearts. You've heard the phrase, "God will often offend the mind to reveal the heart." That's exactly what this is.

Mystery is here to find out if we have another agenda. Is your agenda to figure it all out? Do you have to be in control? Maybe you have to be able to manipulate it to be palatable; to be socially acceptable. Does everybody have to feel good about it? Or are you all right with embracing that which you don't fully understand?

John 8:32 says, "You will know the truth and the truth shall make you free." The word "know" is experiential knowledge. It is truth that has been experienced, not intellectual knowledge. If we don't experience the truth, we'll be limited in our comprehension of it.

God sends the mystery into a service and all of a sudden you don't know why you're crying; you don't know why you're laughing; you don't know why you're shaking; and you don't know why you're feeling lighter. You don't know why you have faith now to believe for what you had formerly been struggling to believe for. The mystery of God comes into a service and you don't know why cancer leaves your body. It is the mystery of God when the Holy Spirit is allowed to move.

Israel never became fruitful; they never fulfilled their destiny. Why? They never overcame the obstacle of rationalism. Rationalism says, "I've got to figure it out." You know some people always use a rationalistic bias whenever they see the move of the Spirit. They don't realize that they're rationalizing away what God wants to release in their lives.

Three enemies to allowing the supernatural to flow are:

1. Failing to deal with our inner "control freak." Ever since we were little kids, we've always wanted to be in control. Even in services we strive for control. I'm finding out that it's good to wait on the Holy Spirit in a service for the mystery to manifest.

In other countries that are experiencing visitations of God, they have a very different sense of time. We ask God to move, but in order to get the full move we've got to come to Mount Sinai. God came to them at Mount Sinai, but they were the ones who chose to back away.

2. The feeding frenzy of social acceptance and the secular mind. We all want to be accepted. The more we feed on this need in an unsanctified way, the more it demands to be fed. Jesus did say that we would be hated on account of Him. He did tell the disciples that when they were rejected to shake off the dust. He gave them instructions on how to handle rejection, and so we should know that we will also be faced with it.

When Jesus told the disciples that He had to go to Jerusalem to die, Peter said, "No, I'm not going to let You die. It's not going to happen." Then Jesus rebuked him, and said, "Get behind Me, satan. You have on your mind the things of men not the things of God."

What Jesus is explaining is that our so-called honorable desires could actually be feeding a strategy of darkness. It's not necessarily because we're thinking something completely demonic; it's because we are thinking something that is man-centered and man-based, which results in a strategy of darkness.

3. Fear of the unknown or that which you can't explain. This is truly an enemy of the supernatural. For these reasons I think the nation of Israel didn't come to the mountain. They desired control and they couldn't explain it. Like them, this is what we've done today; we've chosen predictability over surprise. We've chosen standardization over uniqueness. We'll make every church the same, the same programs and the same service structure. This is the scary thing—we've chosen the natural over the supernatural.

If we were advisors on Mount Sinai, how would we have had God initially reveal Himself for the first timers coming through the door at Mount Sinai Christian Center? Would we have said, "Okay God, don't scare the people away. Make it agreeable to reason, so that everyone can understand what is going on. Make it predictable, palatable, and politically correct. Lord, don't give them too much and blow them away." So what does God do? He blows them away!

I believe that God wanted something in the fiber of their faith; it's the same thing that He wants in the fiber of our Christianity. There is a quality of experience that will release a quantity of results, when you embrace the mystery. There is a quality of an experience that we cannot downsize. There is a harvest that we will receive, if we remain true to the DNA that God put in our spirits.

There's Nothing Like a Good Mystery

To me, who am less than the least of all the saints, this grace was given, that I should preach among the Gentiles the unsearchable riches of Christ, and to make all see what is the fellowship of the mystery, which from the beginning of the ages has been hidden in God who created all things through Jesus Christ (Ephesians 3:8-9).

What does the mystery accomplish?
1. It creates an awe of God that crushes familiarity. We need people to experience the trans-rational, the holy paranormal. I believe

that God wants you to experience the mystery of God because it will create an awe that will crush familiarity.

2. The mystery of God sucks skepticism right out of the atmosphere. Manifestations of the unexplained trigger a new spiritual flow where faith can flourish. A person goes from "it can't happen" to "did you see that?"

3. Establishes a solid testimony. That's what God was doing in Exodus 20. He wanted to establish a testimony. When you encounter a mystery, you remember it. Your encounter with God is to be a mystery that sticks and becomes a solid testimony. It is something that you can hold onto when you go through the thick and thin, when you're seeing the opposite of what God's promised you.

4. It causes a powerful consciousness of divine presence. How many of us have experienced something from God that we couldn't explain? Mysteries upset the equilibrium, and when they upset the equilibrium, God is able to inject truth.

For example, if we were talking to a lost person who thinks they know everything about Christianity, they would already feel like church wasn't for them. As a result, they would most likely go to seek their spirituality elsewhere. But if all of a sudden, the mystery of God manifests on the street of their life, and they received a word of knowledge, or word of wisdom, it would upset the equilibrium of their perception of Christianity. In that moment God would be able to give a heavenly download into their hearts and they would easily get saved.

5. It answers the deep cry of the human heart. Without a mystery our faith deteriorates into religion. If it's explainable, totally understandable, and inside the dimensions of what you can make happen, all you've got is religion.

Religion has no mystery to manifest. That's why a generation is not interested in what we're talking about, because we've been portraying religion. Programmatic evangelism says we need to give them answers. Prophetic evangelism says we need to give them mysteries. We need to do some stuff they can't figure out!

We've been so busy trying to give people answers that we've taken something potent out. We need to let a generation know our God is indescribable! People are tired of religion. They want to see the power of God demonstrated. They want to see the presence of God—blind eyes to see, paralyzed legs to jump out of their wheelchairs. When the Church fails to provide an engaging experience with God, you'll see the youth immediately go to drugs and the occult.

Instead of turning down the volume, we need to turn up the volume. Evangelist Mario Murillo says, "My definition of seeker-sensitive is to turn up the volume so loud that the seeker can sense it!" A modern rock or rap concert is a type of worship experience that the Church often fails to provide. A psychic hot line is a modern spiritual gift experience that the Church in some areas fails to provide.

In this hour, we have a holy obligation to move in a dimension to seize hearts and free them from the mystical mazes of modern life—remember we've got the power!

CHAPTER 10

PROPHETIC EVANGELISM ACTIVATED!

HEALING REVIVALIST JOHN G. LAKE ONCE SAID, "The life of the Christian, without the indwelling power of the Spirit in the heart, is weariness to the flesh."

In Romans 15:18, there is the phrase "in word and deed," which is followed by, "to make the Gentiles obedient." This is the hallmark of the first-century Church when it comes to evangelism. A power-packed gospel went forth in the marketplace and rendered heartfelt salvations in the Book of Acts.

Acts provides a historical narrative of the phenomenal growth of the Church, which directly related to the mighty power of the Spirit, who released signs and wonders through obedient people. In the Book of Acts, we see that each time people were filled with the Holy Spirit, they became powerful, miracle-working, and fruitful evangelists for Christ.

Peter, Philip, and the apostle Paul give us an apostolic view of how to step up, step through, and step into God's redemptive designs. They all operated in the gift of prophecy as they evangelized the lost.

I'm convinced that God still wants to speak directly into the lives of the lost through prophetic phenomena.

In Acts chapter 2, after Peter and the early Church experienced the empowerment of the Spirit, things began to change. Peter went from denying Jesus in front of a "Campfire girl," to boldly proclaiming Christ and testifying of His resurrection. The 120 followers in the upper room

175

experienced the power of the Spirit and were ignited by this baptism of fire. As Peter stood in front of thousands who had gathered outside the upper room, in a strategic way, he began to wear away their defenses to the gospel. Peter told them that the signs and wonders they were experiencing were prophesied by the prophet Joel.

MAKING SENSE

In many places in Scriptures we see prophetic visions, dreams, pictures, impressions, and enigmas used to move people from a place of unbelief to faith.

In Acts 2:22, Peter mentioned the miraculous ministry of Jesus, which was endorsed by God, and followed up by saying "as you yourselves know."

Today, we often want church services that are calm and predictable so we won't have to explain anything to the unchurched guests. Yet what generated the New Testament Church's first major harvest of 2,000 souls was a mystery that required an explanation to the unchurched guests of Jerusalem.

Prophetic evangelism connects what people don't understand about the gospel to what they do understand.

Prophetic evangelism trusts God to unleash "trans-rational" signs to go to work on hearts that are obstinate and minds that are skeptical. Physical healing is a tremendous vehicle for causing hearts to become vulnerable to the gospel. Healing is a physical illustration of a spiritual truth.

In Acts 3, Peter and John stepped into a miracle that arrested the attention of the marketplace where they were functioning.

And a certain man lame from his mother's womb was carried, whom they laid daily at the gate of the temple which is called Beautiful, to ask alms from those who entered the temple; who, seeing Peter and John about to go into the temple, asked for alms. And fixing his eyes on him, with John, Peter said, "Look at us." So he gave them his attention, expecting to receive something from them. Then Peter said, "Silver and gold I do not have, but what I do have I give you: In the name of Jesus Christ of Nazareth, rise up and walk." And he took him by the right hand and lifted him up, and immediately his feet and ankle bones received strength (Acts 3:2-7).

This healing miracle led to 5,000 men coming to Christ (see Acts 4:4). Many times I have seen people come to Christ after God moved by healing someone in the meeting. Even though most Christians would not protest the praying for the sick, few see it as an avenue for mass evangelism.

When Jesus gives the Great Commission in Mark 16:15-18, He begins by telling us to preach the gospel to every creature, and finishes with, among other instructions, "you will take up serpents...." The phrase for "take up" means "to move from its place and to break off attachments." This gives us a more accurate picture of what exploits we will step into.

In prophetic evangelism, we need to be sensitive to the leading of the Holy Spirit. We must let God reveal the root of the problem through revelation (see John 5:19-20). We must be bold, like Peter, to speak and release the anointing and power of God in order to meet the needs of hurting people. Peter seized the miracle, not to promote his own healing ministry, but to declare the matchless message of redemption. That miracle left the people full of amazement and wonder.

NEED TO ENCOUNTER THE DIVINE

Our problem today is that society thinks they have us all figured out. They are not even fazed by our non-demonstration, business-as-usual, religious meetings. They need to encounter the mighty presence of God, which affects people's very lives and destroys the works of the enemy. I think Evangelist Reinhard Bonnke is absolutely correct when he says that "Jesus can only be what you preach Him to be; the Holy Spirit can only bless what you say about Him, and not what you don't say He is." His point is that we must declare Christ to be all that the Bible says He is, so that faith can come for Him to move in that dimension.

We must declare Christ's authority over sin, sickness, and satan! Sometimes that is a scary undertaking, because it goes beyond what flesh can produce. Prophetic evangelism learns to capitalize on the moves and miracles of God in order to communicate Christ's message to reach the unreached.

IF IT CAN HAPPEN TO PETER...

Among those who were empowered by the Spirit, no one personified and utilized the assets of the Spirit more dramatically than Peter. He is a study of contrasts: at times full of faith (see Acts 3:16), at times full of fear (see Mark 14:30), at one time determined (see John 18:10), at another time weak (see Matt. 26:40-45). One moment, he spoke sheer revelation (see Matt. 16:17), the next moment he was a mouthpiece for satan (see Matt. 16:23).

Jesus saw the potential in Simon Peter and gave him the name *Cephas*, meaning "rock." Yet it wasn't until he was filled with the Holy Spirit that Peter's dormant leadership capacity was totally and completely activated. When Peter became empowered by the Spirit, the words of his testimony became immensely effective to his listeners. Under the energizing influence of the Holy Spirit, the global harvest force Jesus initiated through His disciples broke forth into a visible movement.

Over and over again, the history of missions has demonstrated how the public triumph of divine power over evil power was instrumental in expanding the gospel witness. Without this element we fail on two counts. We miss the standard of a pure Christlike witness, and we fall short of meeting the depth of people's needs around us.

IMPOSTOR ALERT

But evil men and impostors will grow worse and worse, deceiving and being deceived (2 Timothy 3:13).

When I think of an impostor, I think of somebody who pretends to be someone they are not, like a deceived person who walks around saying, "I'm Jesus; worship me." But I looked up the word "impostor" in the original, and it means "enchanters using incantations."

Paul is saying that not only will evil get worse and worse, but sorcery and witchcraft will increase. It has been said that right now in America, the enlistment and recruitment of teenagers into Wicca and the occult is rising. We could lose our nation if we don't decide to change! On the flip side, I've never seen as many people come to the Lord as I have seen recently. People are more hungry for Christ than they have ever been before!

CONSEQUENCES OF A *DUNAMIS* DEFAULT

A dunamis default is a crisis of epic proportions. What happens if the people of God don't release the life of the gospel?

In Acts 8, there was a man by the name of Simon the Sorcerer. He went to Samaria, where nearly the entire town gave heed to him. They called him the "Great Power of God." But he was an imposter. He was passing himself off to be someone who embodied God.

But there was a certain man called Simon, who previously practiced sorcery in the city and astonished the people of Samaria, claiming that he was someone great, to whom they all gave heed, from the least to the greatest, saying, "This man is the great power of God," And they heeded him because he had astonished them with his sorceries for a long time (Acts 8:9-11).

Samaria is very much like our world today. We can sit back and complain when there is a high tech séance program on TV, but the reason it is there is because of our default. People believe there is more power in the séance show than in the lives of believers. I've heard it said: All it takes for evil to advance is for good men to do nothing. Passivity during this time is criminal.

In Acts chapter 8, you can read the story of a deacon in the early Church named Philip. We're told that his job was to wait on tables. He literally served food and met the needs of widows, so the other apostles could go out preaching.

So when God wants to turn a city around we might think He would get a superstar apostle, right? No, because God says, "I'm going to get a glorified drink waiter who has been faithful doing what I have called him to do." Here is Philip; one day he's taking orders from widows, the next day he's taking cities from devils.

DUNAMIS IN REVERSE

You might wonder, what happens if an inexperienced man like Philip doesn't demonstrate the dunamis power of God? All of these people are blindly following the sorcerer Simon, but when they see the power of God on Philip, they turn, confess, and believe in Christ and get water baptized.

What happens if Philip doesn't go?

And the multitudes with one accord heeded the things spoken by Philip, hearing and seeing the miracles which he did. For unclean spirits, crying with a loud voice, came out of many who were possessed; and many who were paralyzed and lame were healed. And there was great joy in that city (Acts 8:6-8).

A dunamis default means that if you don't walk in the power of the Holy Spirit, there will be no multitude listening to what you have to say. The consequence of a dunamis default is that the crowd we're meant to speak to will never hear us. What about the miracles that are meant to take place that don't take place all because we don't get there? There are miracles in motion that God has designated, but He is waiting for someone who will say in obedience, "I'll go there."

If unclean spirits don't come out, they stay in. Unclean spirits are tied to perversion. The rise of sorcery will also mean the rise of perversion, because they go hand in hand. Notice that the Word doesn't say they had a chemical imbalance or a bad childhood. No, it says they were "possessed." The word *possessed* means to "retain under grip." Our diagnosis must be accurate for our prognosis to meet the challenge.

If unclean spirits don't come out, people would stay under the grip of darkness, though they could have been set free. There would be no healing. People would stay in sicknesses and bondage in their bodies. Not only would the demonic be controlling their spirit, emotionally and mentally tormenting them, but also striking them physically.

And finally, if you don't have joy, you have depression. Without Philip's obedience to demonstrating the gospel, there would have been no joy released in the city.

FORFEITING *DUNAMIS* IN A CITY

Let's take any city today and say that the people who need to be filled with the Holy Ghost don't get filled. And the people who are already filled with the Holy Ghost don't go out and do what God directs them to do. What happens? They forfeit dunamis power in that city.

But Philip, who is not even an apostle, goes right out and undertakes spiritual warfare. People talk about warfare being prayer, and I believe that you've got to pray, but do you know what spiritual warfare is also? The proclamation of the gospel. We don't speak about that often, but what Philip accomplished in that city was spiritual warfare. Warfare is not just praying in a back room; it is preaching Christ in the marketplace. It is vital that we take God's answers to our prayers, get up off of our knees, and go tell people what God has said!

Several years earlier, Jesus walked out to a well in Samaria (see John 4). He was directed not to preach to a major crowd, but to one particular Samaritan woman. Jesus had this encounter with her for the purpose of giving her a word of knowledge, and offering to her everlasting water. She is so amazed at His accuracy about the details of her life that she runs back into Samaria to tell everyone about it. The Bible says that she tells the city, "You've got to see this man! He's told me everything!" Almost the entire city came out to hear Jesus that day and they believed.

FROM AWAKENING TO BEWITCHED TO INFILLING

Now let's go back to the Book of Acts, about three years later. How can you go from a citywide awakening to only three years later where a sorcerer has an entire city bewitched and following after him? All of those folks who experienced that awakening didn't die in the span of three years. I started thinking about this concept of a dunamis default. There are only two possible explanations that I could think of about how there could be a mighty move of God, followed by amazing deception, where people are blinded and possessed.

One scenario is the people who went out and heard Jesus never said anything to anyone else. In other words, the miracle was never broadcasted. They kept to themselves. A second scenario is that they became believers but remained baby Christians and never grew up. You know when you're a baby Christian, it's "all about me." You're cool with everything revolving around you because you're still a baby.

But when people are much older, and you still have to feed and clothe them, it's not so cool anymore. When pastors have to clean up adult messes, it's not cute. Maybe there's another explanation, but somewhere along the line it seems like they were either silent, or they turned inward.

Philip realized he couldn't just leave these converts on their own as new believers. They had tasted the supernatural realm of the demonic and now they needed to taste the supernatural realm of the divine! They needed to be filled with the Holy Spirit. So Philip called on Peter and John. If you keep reading in Acts chapter 8, Peter and John come down and they pray for the Samaritan believers and they receive the Holy Spirit. There was evidence that it was broadcasted. God saw to it that this time Samaria was filled with the Holy Spirit.

MESSY CONVERSIONS

When I was a student at the University of the Pacific, I was involved in a campus ministry. I was very young in the Lord. I came back from a Sunday night service where the man who had discipled me had preached a mighty message about Peter getting out of the boat.

At that time, I had a neighbor named Vincent, who was a very imposing figure. He was six feet four inches tall, weighed 260 pounds, and was a very disturbed man. In fact, he was on medication and was an outpatient from the local mental hospital. He was on State Disability because he couldn't get a job in his condition. When I came back from this meeting, I told my roommate, "We've got to witness to Vincent. We just need to do it. It's time." But my roommate said, "Brother, that's crazy. I'm not going over there."

I walked next door and knocked on his door. Vincent answered the door and his eyes looked funny. He let me in, but I could tell he was angry. He said, "Hold on a second," and he went into his bedroom.

I stood there in his apartment looking around. On one side of the room was a picture of a skeleton with a snake coming out of its mouth.

On the other side was a picture of a flying dragon with two daggers in its claws. I looked in the corner of his kitchen and there was a machete with what looked like dried blood on it. The devil started lying to me by saying that the blood belonged to the last dude who tried to come in to witness to him.

I thought it wasn't a good time because I heard Vincent talking to someone in his bedroom. I walked over and peeked into his bedroom to say, "Hey, man, I'll come back another time when you're not busy," but no one was there with him. He was talking to an old war buddy who had died years before in his arms. (Okay, now I'm officially freaked.)

All of a sudden, I thought, "I've got to conquer this thing." So I said to him, "Hey, Vincent, I've got to talk to you. You need the Lord, man. Jesus Christ can change your life. We need to pray right now." I just grabbed his hands and didn't give him a chance to say anything. I got to the part where I normally say, "Jesus is Lord" and the moment he went to say Jesus, he started choking and growling violently. He started roaring and squeezing my hands so hard that I couldn't move. At that point, I opened my eyes. (I've since learned that when you pray with people who have "visitors on board," you shouldn't close your eyes.)

I looked up at his red face, and his eyes were rolled back into his head. "Oh, my God, this is not good," was all I could think. I wanted to pull my hands loose so I could knock on the wall, hoping my roommate would hear and dial 9-1-1, but I couldn't. In that moment, I didn't know what would happen, so I thought my only chance was to come against this power of darkness. I raised my voice and said, "In the name of Jesus, I break this power and command you to let him go right now!" His eyes popped back, he started looking at me, and he asked, "What just happened?"

I prayed with him for Jesus to come into his life and he got baptized in the Holy Ghost. Vincent started coming out to Bible studies, church, carrying a Bible, got a job, got off of medication, and was released from the mental hospital. His life was totally transformed in a moment!

I was just a student in campus ministry, young in the Lord, and I definitely lacked experience. I believe we are going into a time in this world where we're going to see a huge jump in these types of conversions!

HELL'S RED BUTTON

For the kingdom of God is not in word but in power (1 Corinthians 4:20).

One night I was sleeping in my bed and I suddenly woke up at about 2:30 A.M. I sensed God speaking to me, "I want you to be on guard because a spirit of witchcraft is going to be coming against your house, your family, your children, and your ministry."

Witchcraft/sorcery is the equivalent to the President's rumored nuclear "red button." It becomes hell's last ditch effort to frantically thwart God's rising move amongst His children.

With the king of Moab (see 2 Kings 3:26-27), and Balak (see Num. 24:1,10), these instances portray the extremes to which wicked instruments will utilize witchcraft to fight against the expansion of the people of God.

So I jumped out of bed and I started to anoint our doors. I looked for the anointing oil, but we didn't have any, so I used Crisco oil. (I guess oil is oil.) I recognized that God doesn't warn you about the "wimpy" attacks at 2:30 in the morning.

PROPHETIC VERSUS PSYCHIC

I often preach at U.C.-Berkeley, a college campus that is known for its rebellion and protesting. There is a man whom I've had some run-ins with and he called himself "the Hate Man of Berkeley." Every time I went to preach or went out on the campus to do an outreach—advertised or not—this guy would find me.

Years ago, I went to Berkeley for a prayer walk with my wife and kids and some college students. As we were praying, I noticed there were some students dressed like vampires carrying sacks of blood. They were pasty-faced, and everything about them was dark.

So I walked over to a guy and asked, "What are you doing?" He replied, "We're role playing, and I'm a vampire, and all of our friends are vampires. The idea of the game is to kill the other person and drink their blood, but it's just for fun." (How about playing Yahtzee, Pictionary, or something?)

At that same time, we heard wild drums beating. We went over to the middle of the university center and there were students gathered all around. They were beating hollowed out industrial drums with broken sticks. They were also chanting some mantra. The moment I walked past, I could feel a demonic presence. I knew immediately I had to witness to these guys—I couldn't just walk by there and not say anything. This would be the first time I would meet him: the Hate Man of Berkeley. As soon as my friend, Jeff Rostocil, and I, turned the corner after dropping my family off at the car, they were gone. I mean it was like turning a light on inner-city cockroaches—they had scattered. Only a couple of people remained, and one of them was the Hate Man.

I walked over to him and said "Hey, man, my name is Sean, and I just wanna…" He interrupted me, put up his hands, and said, "Don't talk to me unless you put your hands on my hands and say, 'I hate you.'" This is why he's called the Hate Man. He supposedly gets empowered when you put your hands on his hands and say, "I hate you." I looked back at him and said, "I'm here to tell you that Jesus Christ wants your life."

He got visibly upset and jumped back from me. Right next to us was one of the young guys who had been beating the drums. We ended up witnessing to this young man and praying with him for salvation right on the spot. Needless to say, I was not the Hate Man's friend from that point on. I had now taken one of his disciples.

A Different Kind of Blue Light Special

So, let me fast forward. I'm doing another prayer walk with a college ministry that's on the same campus. As we're talking and saying good-bye, I notice the Hate Man and he's watching me from a distance. I glanced over at him, not too concerned. But he had something like a blue laser in his hand.

I see him flash this blue light, but I'm not really paying attention to him. In that moment, when I noticed the blue light, I turned to say something to someone and it felt like someone had taken a mallet and hit me right on the back of my head. Immediately, I collapsed on my knees and I was holding my head. It felt like a blood vessel was bursting in my brain. I felt like I was dying.

My son was the only one to recognize what was going on and said "Dad, what's going on? What's the matter?" I said, "Son, I don't know." I was ready to tell him to call 9-1-1 when all of a sudden, the Lord spoke to me and said, "A spirit of witchcraft is coming against you now and I want you to bind it." I said, "In the name of Jesus, I bind this spirit of witchcraft!"

As soon as I did that, it lifted as suddenly as it had come on me. I stood right back on my feet and it was like nothing had happened. The moment I did, I turned and looked over to where the Hate Man was.

He started shaking and dropped that little blue light. I started walking toward him. He picked it up and started to walk away. Though I am an evangelist, and a minister, I'm still from inner city Oakland, and if you're going to cast a curse on me, I'm going to cast the devil out of you! I started running after him and he just took off.

WHERE'S YOUR POWER SOURCE?

Now a certain woman named Lydia heard us. She was a seller of purple from the city of Thyatira, who worshiped God. The Lord opened her heart to heed the things spoken by Paul. And when she and her household were baptized, she begged us, saying, "If you have judged me to be faithful to the Lord, come to my house and stay." So she persuaded us. Now it happened, as we went to prayer, that a certain slave girl possessed with a spirit of divination met us, who brought her masters much profit by fortune-telling. This girl followed Paul and us, and cried out, saying, "These men are the servants of the Most High God, who proclaim to us the way of salvation." And this she did for many days. But Paul, greatly annoyed, turned and said to the spirit, "I command you in the name of Jesus Christ to come out of her." And he came out that very hour (Acts 16:14-18).

So Paul went to a place called Philippi and he happened upon a lady by the name of Lydia. They were having a nice little time at the riverside, and the Bible tells us that the Lord had opened her heart to heed the things spoken by Paul. He prayed with her, she was baptized, and there you have the birth of the Philippian church. (Wouldn't it be great if everyone you ever witnessed to was like that? It was nice, clean, and tidy.) Then Paul crossed over the river, and now look what happened. Notice the contrast. Paul and Silas are going to prayer, but the people of Philippi are going to see a psychic, the girl with a spirit of divination.

What I submit to you is that at this time in history there is a move from nice and easy conversions, to "messy" conversions where we're going to encounter the demonic realm. We're going to come up against folks who have visitors on board (times when you look into someone's eyes and other beings are looking back).

That is our generation today. People are tapping into other power sources, saying it's not enough to just have natural abilities. People are finding that what they are used to isn't useful to them anymore. Folks are saying, "I've got to tap into the supernatural realm."

If you believe in Jesus Christ, you had better be praying. You had better be tapping into your Power Source. Now is not the time to have some sort of limp-wristed, houseplant Christianity. Now is the time to have an empowered, Holy Ghost walk with God, where you walk in a dimension of authority and power! Instead of getting up in the morning and reaching for headache tablets because the devil makes you afraid, you get up and the devil has to reach for his headache tablets.

I've come to realize that curses are going to a whole new level. There are people all around this nation in rituals going to the next level in the demonic. Paul operated in the prophetic weapon of discernment and was alert to the nature and strategies of the enemy.

God and satan have virtually nothing in common, but this one thing: God and satan can both invest power into people. Satan's power is no comparison to God's power, because God has ultimate power!

CUTTING OFF THE AIR SUPPLY

When I was a kid I used to go down to the swimming pool and I had a big ol' 'fro. These guys at the pool would grab us (younger kids) and hold us by our hair under the water. We would be struggling and trying to fight and they would hold us down until we stopped fighting. We would come up for air and they would stick us back under. All the lifeguards were into each other, so they didn't even notice us little inner-city kids getting dunked. In similar fashion, the enemy wants to hold you under.

The demonic realm wants to spiritually suffocate a person. People want to come up for air; they want to come up for joy; they want to come up for liberty, but they are being held under.

I believe it wasn't just any coincidence that the devil didn't want this girl to meet Paul and Silas. I think in her heart she wanted to be free, and it was a moment where she came up breathing for a second, only to be pushed back down again. So how did the girl get there? The only way that this teenaged girl got to the place where she was being gripped, seized, and retained is that somewhere along the line she closed the door to God and opened the wrong door. Having a persistent adversary and opening the wrong spiritual door is where this generation is finding themselves.

The Bible says that the girl with the spirit of divination "met us." The word "met" means a face-to-face encounter. I believe that this generation of believers is also going to have face-to-face encounters with the demonic.

The *spirit of divination*, in the original text, means "a python spirit." One of the clues of how the spirit of divination works is found in this snake. How does a python kill? It wraps itself around and around, and every time the victim inhales, it tightens its grasp. When the victim goes to breathe in again and get some more air, it continues to choke him. The snake cuts off its air supply.

What a spirit of divination wants to do is cut off a generation from the breath of Christ! That is why there are kids who are so angry at God and so bitter, or in such unbelief that all they can see is darkness; the enemy has wrapped itself around them.

The practice of witchcraft has dramatically increased in recent years and here is one of the express goals of this movement: "To dilute, dominate, and destroy biblical Christianity."

Ultimately, Paul saw this girl delivered and allowed the demonstration of truth to be seen in Philippi.

"A HUNTING THEY WILL GO..."

Thus says the Lord God: "Woe to the women who sew magic charms on their sleeves and make veils for the heads of people of every height to hunt souls! Will you hunt the souls of My people, and keep yourselves alive?" ...Therefore thus says the Lord God: "Behold, I am against your magic charms by which you hunt souls there like birds. I will tear them from your arms, and let the souls go, the souls you hunt like birds" (Ezekiel 13:18,20).

The real damage in sorcery is its ability to "veil" people. This spirit doesn't want you to see right or clearly. It doesn't want you to understand what's really at stake. It says it makes veils; it hunts souls. This spirit is aggressive! It wants souls, but God declares freedom over captives. Peter, Philip, and Paul demonstrate for the prophetic evangelist how to aggressively compete for the souls of lost humanity.

LESSONS FROM THE "ACTIVATED"

Each of these three examples from the Book of Acts reveals tremendous principles for modern prophetic evangelists. In these instances, Peter, Philip, and Paul conquer the opposition while seeing a harvest released! They operated in the power of the Spirit as they stepped out to win souls.

Professor of cross-cultural communications, Del Tarr, says, "Aspects of revival convinced me that some of satan's territory cannot be penetrated without the power of the Holy Spirit in signs and wonders."

The Peter Factor

"The Peter Factor" is receiving the Spirit's power to be a witness. After receiving the Baptism of the Holy Spirit, Peter found himself engaging the unchurched in the marketplace. He got out of the upper room and out on the streets. Any and every experience with the Spirit of God must lead us eventually toward God's redemptive purposes.

In Acts 4:4, Peter saw another 5,000 get saved. Prophetic evangelism manifested in both an outpouring followed by evangelism and a gift of healing followed by evangelism. These conversions underscore the importance of Spirit-driven (prophetic) evangelism.

The Peter Factor is stepping out to pray for the sick in the market-place and giving God the glory. It also speaks of total penetration as the disciples spread the gospel wherever they went.

The Philip Factor

Philip was faithful to preach Christ to Samaria. As a result he saw God confirm the Word with signs following. Philip emphasized miracle evangelism to reach Samaria. He was faithful in mass evangelism, but he needed Peter and John's help to pray for the Samaritans' to receive the Holy Spirit. Philip was willing to leave a move of God to step into a divine appointment with a man of Ethiopia. This Ethiopian happened to be reading Isaiah and needed some answers.

The Philip Factor is where there will be times we need to have additional giftings to complete some assignments. Christian editor, Jim Buchan says, "It's time to reconnect apostolic and prophetic ministries to their original calling to equip the Church for winning a lost world." The Philip Factor also emphasizes the boldness to go into hostile territory to deliver souls. Finally, the Philip Factor is the willingness to engage people one-on-one, by the leading of God, which releases supernatural transformations.

The Paul Factor

Paul stepped into Philippi having to compete with the spirit of divination. He dealt with it head on and received persecution over it. This backlash issue led to Paul being imprisoned, where he praised God and led a Philippian jailer to the Lord. This was the birth of the Philippian church. Paul even got the city magistrate to parade them out of prison, when the magistrates wanted him to leave town secretly.

The Paul Factor aggressively competes for souls because the spirit of witchcraft is actively hunting for souls. The Paul Factor is also about outlasting backlash and looking for a platform to win souls. Paul didn't wallow in his set backs but saw them as divine set ups to proclaim Christ to a lost world.

Finally, the Paul Factor is about not slipping out secretly, but letting our light shine despite our situations. Paul made sure the gospel had a hearing, even if he had to stay in a collapsed prison until his reluctant escorts came to usher him out. Demonstrating and imparting the supernatural dimension of the kingdom of God is so crucial in this hour. The Book of Acts highlights the missing ingredient in traditional evangelism, which is prophetic power; thus modeling a standard that calls forth prophetic evangelists.

ACTION STEP ADDENDUM
DREAMS AND VISIONS—ACTIVATED!

When Peter stood up on the day of Pentecost, he quoted from the prophet Joel declaring a new era had begun. Joel promised that an era would come where dreams and visions would be widespread in the earth saying, "Your sons and daughters shall prophesy, your old men will dream dreams, your young men will see visions..." (Acts 2:17b).

Dreams and visions were a significant part of God's means of communication to humanity in Scriptures; Strong's Concordance lists 202 references to these manifestations in the Bible. While there are counterfeits, imitations, and some well-meaning people in error, God still has the genuine article. In Job 33:13, we are told that God will seal instructions in people's hearts using dreams to direct them with this prophetic phenomenon. Apostle Paul experienced what Job talked about. During the night Paul had a vision of a man of Macedonia imploring him to come there and minister (see Acts 16:9).

There have been some critical times in which God has directed, alerted, or highlighted a course of action for my wife, children, and me through a dream or vision. While we must be very discerning, and test the revelation, we must also be careful not to throw out the baby with the bath water.

I'm intrigued about how God set up the Gentile Pentecost (see Acts 10) by sending a heavenly messenger to Cornelius, a centurion, and a vision to Peter while he took a nap on a roof. The result was a divine connection between these two heavyweights, and mighty salvations and empowerments among these Gentiles. This instigated a bold new step in the missions of the Church from that point on.

Many times I've heard firsthand testimonies of how missionaries and evangelists were prophetically directed to ripe areas and then saw amazing conversions. One missionary told me of accounts where Muslim people have been converted through these prophetic dreams and visions.

In Scripture, God sometimes spoke through dreams to lost people. God gave dreams to Pharaoh (see Gen. 41:1-7), Nebuchadnezzar (see Dan. 4:5), the wise men (see Matt. 2:12), and Pilate's wife (see Matt. 27:19). I'm convinced that this subject will become more prevalent and could open doors for us to minister the gospel to lost souls. In this post modern generation this is very catchy and will speak volumes to them. So we need to be in touch with them, and become close with the Holy Spirit to see this avenue mined for God's glory in a massive harvest of souls.

Begin to seek God to reveal His directions to you through all of the means of Scripture, and that He would work on unbelievers day and night to bring them to repentance.

CHAPTER 11

SPIRITUAL AUTHORITY AND THE DUNAMIS LIFESTYLE

SUCCESSFUL MINISTRY IS BASED UPON not only knowing what Jesus has done for us, but who He has made us to be. God has given us position and enabling which flows from our very being. Jesus intends that we have the divine release of spiritual authority and walk in the dunamis (power) lifestyle. Christ designed a total defeat of hell's dark powers and has authorized you and me to enforce it.

The Disciples of Christ have marching orders in the Great Commission, which include giving spiritual light and destroying works of darkness. To break people free from sickness, brokenness, and demonization is on course with God's purposes. Thus, we can minister with confidence and expect God's release as we step out to accomplish these orders.

In Luke 9:1-2 it says, "He [Jesus] called His twelve...and gave them authority over all demons, and to cure diseases. He sent them to preach the kingdom of God." We've been given an authority to partner with God to bring good news to people, to break bondages off of people, and to restore God's blessing. We've been given spiritual authority to deal with spiritual problems.

Now more than ever, a new enabling—grace—is needed to win the lost. We need something that is beyond our ability to persuade and reach people. We need God to put His hand on us, so that it will go beyond having good beliefs, to rescuing souls for eternity.

193

Many Christians have felt spiritually powerless. They feel the loss of Christian influence, yet God is looking for partners who walk in a new dimension of authority. Professor Charles Kraft says, "The purpose for which God gives us this authority is to use it to imitate Jesus." We must act on His behalf.

> *And He said to them, "Go into all the world and preach the gospel to every creature. He who believes and is baptized will be saved; but he who does not believe will be condemned. And these signs will follow those who believe: In My name they will cast out demons; they will speak with new tongues; they will take up serpents; and if they drink anything deadly, it will by no means hurt them; they will lay hands on the sick, and they will recover"* (Mark 16:15-18).

The Great Commission was not just about words. Jesus said that signs were going to follow those words. In Jesus' culture, stories were passed down from generation to generation, but He was saying that there would not just be stories, but physical signs. I don't want to be satisfied with simply retelling a story of what God did in the past. If all we do is sit back and talk about what other great people have done in the past, we're missing the mark.

If we're believers, Jesus said these signs should follow us. If we have the Holy Spirit in our lives, there is no reason that we shouldn't be living a dunamis lifestyle. Here is my desire: a new dimension of spiritual exploits; I yearn to see something more than I've ever seen or heard.

IT'S IN OUR DNA

When I first came to Christ, I would hear the word *revival* quite often. I was immediately captivated and intrigued by this word. The reason I was attracted to revival was twofold: (1) I intuitively realized God is glorified in revival. The human heart is captivated in revival more than any other time, and (2) I believe that God was putting a particular DNA in my spirit. It was like I was saying in my heart, "God, whatever this thing is, I want to see it, I want to be in it." Here I am almost two decades later and I'm still saying, "I want revival."

Dr. C. Peter Wagner, founder of Wagner Leadership Institute, detected that over the years there has been a "gradual de-emphasizing of signs, wonders, and other miraculous ministries." We cannot settle for a miracle-free Christianity! Don't settle for a Christianity that you can figure out and a walk where you don't have to trust God to do something miraculous. Don't simply rely on human effort, or a mutant version of Christianity. Let's believe daily for God to do something out of the ordinary in our lives and the lives around us.

The key to experiencing the miracle-working power of God is listening and obeying in faith, the instructions of the Father. God's purpose for working miracles is to demonstrate His love and power to the non-churched, and to destroy the works of the enemy.

OPEN FOR BUSINESS

And he called his ten servants, and delivered them ten pounds, and said unto them, "Occupy till I come" (Luke 19:13 KJV).

The word *occupy* is a military term. To occupy something doesn't mean to sit in the pew of a church, but an occupational force is put strategically in place. After the war is won, the occupational force remains so pockets of resistance can be terminated. God has put you as an occupational force on planet earth. We have been given authority on this planet to rise up and fight the pockets of spiritual resistance that come against our King's intentions. The war has already been won on Calvary. It's over! But the story continues in us, because the Bible says that God is going to crush satan underneath our feet (see Rom. 16:20). Occupy also means to do business. We've got to step into the Father's business. The Father's business is about redemption and saving souls; it is a supernatural business.

The supernatural is the technology of the spiritual future. God demands this so He would be represented by more than just mere words. God is not a philosophy; He is not a concept. God is saying that what is required to be a witness in this hour is that we have a dunamis lifestyle and not just lip service.

Getting the Leverage of the Lord

In Exodus 4, Moses is working for his father-in-law on the back-side of the desert. But all of a sudden a bush is on fire in front of him and begins to speak to him!

Through that burning bush, God speaks to Moses about delivering His people. Moses was probably thinking, "Okay God, you've given me a pretty heavy assignment." Pharaoh had the strongest known military army of his day. So Moses says, "Why should Pharaoh listen to me?" And God asks, "What's in your hand, son?" Moses looks at his hand, "A stick." So here's the deal, God's going to send a man with a stick to Pharaoh, and tell him to let God's people go. Moses was probably wondering, "Do You want me to hit the man with the stick?"

Now you shall speak to him and put the words in his mouth. And I will be with your mouth and with his mouth, and I will teach you what you shall do. So he shall be your spokesman to the people. And he himself shall be as a mouth for you, and you shall be to him as God (Exodus 4:15-16).

God was telling Moses, "You're going to say what you've always said but when I breathe on your words, they're going to carry more weight. The Egyptians will remember your words in the night hours; they will continue running through their minds. I will capture their attention. You're going to be the deliverer, but I'm going to be the One behind you."

Moses was given an epic assignment, but his temptation was to shrink back. The Great Commission is an epic assignment. Like Moses, our temptation is to shrink back from our assignment, because we don't feel we've been furnished with everything that we need to accomplish the task. Moses said, "Why should they listen to me?" His question reflected his hesitancy. "What evidence can I produce that I'm on a divine mission? How can I prove to that man that I actually met with You?" Good questions.

When the rod became a snake and then became a rod again in Moses' hands, God got his attention. It was as if God was saying, "You're not going with just any stick. You point this thing at the water, and oceans will part."

Gordon Lindsey once said, "Every person called to ministry must decide what their attitude will be toward the supernatural." Moses definitely developed a positive attitude towards God's manifestation of the supernatural. He would not have survived without the supernatural.

If our enemy has an AK-47 and we know we're going to be fighting against him, we don't come out with some small rocks in our hands. Even if we hit the guy with the rocks, he's not going down. That is equivalent to throwing humanistic arguments against the deception that locks up students on campuses. We can't throw out our own little opinions while the enemy is using AK-47s. We've got to have a rod that wields spiritual leverage.

What is spiritual leverage? It is a combination of the mind of Christ and the authority of Christ, both of which God has made available to you and me. You can move anything if you have enough leverage. You may have a massive boulder, but if you have enough leverage, you can move it.

> *For it is impossible for those who were once enlightened, and have tasted the heavenly gift, and have become partakers of the Holy Spirit, and have tasted the good word of God and the powers of the age to come...* (Hebrews 6:4-5).

Now here is part of the leverage. God wants us to taste from the power of an age to come. We're to walk in it because God has made it available to us. Part of the heavenly gift is tasting of the age to come. The dunamis lifestyle is walking in the power of an age that is not yet fully here.

UNDERSTANDING THE ROD

In the days of old, a rod meant several important things: (1) It was the symbol of authority (Revelation 2:27 discusses reigning with the rod of authority) and for Moses it represented the shepherd's call; (2) it was used by Moses to walk with, lean on, and protect him, and (3) scholars tell us that shepherds would write and carve figures on their rods.

The rod was like a journal of past life experiences. God asked Moses, "What's that in your hand?" To him it symbolized the authority that he currently walked in. There were probably some carved images on this rod, a journal of important things that had happened in his life. And God said, "Throw it down." If Moses was going to deal with skepticism and tentativeness, he was going to need some authority in Egypt.

The dunamis lifestyle is about the authority of the believer that God has deposited inside of you. If you only understood the power of His Spirit inside of you, you would walk in the authority that could move mountains. The more you know who you are in Christ, the more you will work in harmony with the Holy Spirit. You will be able to tap into the riches of Christ when you can truly see what God has deposited inside of you.

God told Moses to make sure that he did all those wonders that God had put in his hand (see Exod. 4:21). The rod which God had Moses take up was representative of a conferring of authority. Many Christians today never utilize their rod, leaving the wonders that God put in their hands unused.

In order for you to step into the dunamis lifestyle, sometimes you've got to throw down some things that you've previously leaned upon. Generally, people find that God is stronger in them when they surrender to Him, or when they're in a position of weakness before God. Your past history, good or bad, must be willingly laid down. Lay it all down and pick up the rod of dunamis power that God wants to give you. You cannot pick up God's rod with hands that are already full; you've got to empty them.

OPERATING FROM HEAVEN'S VANTAGE POINT

Jesus was exalted to a name that is above every other name. Jesus' name is above every principality, every power, any earthly king or government, and over anything in the spirit realm. When you are born again, you are seated immediately in heavenly places, regardless of your earthly position. We are in Christ, so if Jesus is in heavenly places, above all principalities, that's where we are also. When you are operating as an obedient believer, you're not operating from ground level; you're operating from a heavenly level.

Moses' rod became a serpent. A serpent was the symbol of royal and cultic powers. A serpent was placed on the diadem of every Pharaoh because it was the mark of sovereignty.

Then God says, "I want you to take the serpent by the tail." Most of us have never handled snakes, but common sense says you ought to grab it by the head so that it can't turn around and bite you. God was testing the man. Moses was a little tentative reaching out, but the moment he grabbed the snake, it became a rod again. God was showing Moses that He was going to give him authority. One of the Egyptians' gods was a serpent and God was clearly showing Moses He would give him power over their gods.

This experience gave Moses two illustrations to furnish him with boldness and become a catalyst to his mission:

1. The sign of the rod. The conquered snake became a rod of authority in Moses' hands. This illustrates the miracle of conversion. The rod was converted and Moses would also see a nation converted. God wants you to know that the authority and power for massive conversions has been released to you! Miracles of conversions ought to be the order of the day. We will see former "snakes" (people who have been bound) become instruments of deliverance in the Master's hand.

2. The sign of the cleansed hand. In Exodus 4:6-7, Moses' hand became leprous and then was miraculously healed and returned to normal. This illustrates the miracle of restoration. The gospel releases power to see restored lives, relationships, dreams, and the ability to walk forward into God's plan.

God has given us the privilege to witness the restoration of what the devil has stolen from people. As you step out, you will see that restoration of people's peace, health, freedom, and their very lives await you. The dunamis lifestyle is walking in authority and not being apologetic or fearful. It is seeing through eternal eyes that you have royal placement. If you follow Christ, you are an ambassador of the entire kingdom of God on earth.

Most assuredly, I say to you, he who believes in Me, the works that I do he will do also; and greater works than these he will do, because I go to My Father (John 14:12).

It is impossible for the spirit realm to turn a deaf ear to you when you know the power of your words. When you know the spiritual power within you, the spirit realm always hears.

All authority lives in us, but because there is also resistance in us, we don't see that power. Power flows where authority is released and that is why we can't talk about witnessing without talking about authority. We've been limited in our power and felt powerless because some of it is connected to not knowing the authority we have in Christ.

HE'S FALLEN AND HE CAN'T GET UP

Then the seventy returned with joy, saying "Lord, even the demons are subject to us in Your name.... Nevertheless do not rejoice in this, that the spirits are subject to you, but rather rejoice because your names are written in Heaven" (Luke 10:17,20).

Jesus keeps this exploit in perspective and says, "I saw satan fall like lightning. But even more important than this, you need to be excited that your names are written in the Lamb's Book of Life." Jesus makes the connection about where the power flows. It's not just you who the devil is afraid of; it is the One who stands behind you. This delegated authority is also connected to His redemptive purpose.

HUMAN ASSOCIATION VERSUS DIVINE ASSOCIATION

Then some of the itinerant Jewish exorcists took it upon themselves to call the name of the Lord Jesus over those who had evil spirits, saying, "We exorcise you by the Jesus whom Paul preaches." Also there were seven sons of Sceva, a Jewish chief priest, who did so (Acts 19:13-14).

In Acts chapter 19, verse 14, seven sons of a Jewish priest found a guy who was demonized and tried to exorcise the demons out of him. (This guy was a walking Bermuda-triangle—filled with demons.)

The Jewish priests evidently had some authority because the sons of Sceva must have thought authority from God works like hand-me-downs. They didn't realize that you have to have your own walk with God, because ultimately the enemy is going to check you out and see what your connection with God is. The standout phrase in this passage is "they took it upon themselves." These seven sons of the Jewish priest took it upon themselves to exorcise this demonic entity. That tells me they didn't have authentic authority from God. There's a big difference between human association and divine association.

We've all heard the saying, "It's not what you know but who you know." It's all about who you have an intimate relationship with. Divine association is what furnishes you with supernatural adequacy. Daniel 11:32 tells us that if we know God, we will be used mightily, and step forth with great exploits.

These seven sons had no authentic connection with God. They walk up to this man and say, "We exorcize you by the Jesus whom Paul preaches." The demons that were inside the man got riled up by what they said. The demons state that they knew Jesus and Paul, "but who are you?" The demonized man beat up each of the seven sons and they all ran out of the house naked and bleeding.

In contrast—the 70 disciples in Luke 10 came back with an experience in dealing with demonic entities, confronting powers and seeing people get set free. They came back with joy. Seven others guys are running around without any clothes on. They're not excited; they're not joyful—they're exposed. The issue then and now is authentic authority.

Spiritual Authority Consists of Certain Components:

1. Spiritual authority is being recognized by God (see Acts 2:22). Your ability to navigate the challenges of this life is largely based on whether or not you're recognized by God.

Here's what the demons inside of the man had said before he beat up the seven sons, "Jesus I know, Paul I know, but who are you?" (Acts 19:15). If a "visitor on board" speaks to someone and says, "I know Jesus, and I know Joe, but who are you?," it's time to turn and run because you're about to get beat up. The moral of the story is to have a relationship with God when you go into these situations.

We can learn something else from the seven sons who ran down the street bleeding and naked (see Acts 19:16). Naked means they were exposed. The truth of the matter is that we are living in a time today when folks are going to get exposed. It's symbolized by their running, fleeing from their problems, fleeing from the situation that has gotten out of hand—they're exposed.

2. Spiritual authority is a transfer of government, influence, and power from God. It is as if Heaven is an ATM machine for those who walk with God. If you have relationship with Christ, you have the access code, and everything that is in the kingdom you can access in the name of Jesus Christ.

There's a spiritual ATM machine when you drop on your knees and you've got the current access code. The slip comes out and it says in the account whatever it is that you had extracted and the amount still left.

But no matter how much you extract, your account is still full because the kingdom can never be depleted. When you come to Christ, He transfers to your account authority and power in His name.

3. Spiritual authority includes a specific commission from God. It's amazing how many people want more of the anointing, but they don't want to take on the assignments of God. They want to have the signs and wonders (see Mark 16), but they don't like the rest of the verse, "Go into all the world." Authority rests on those who use the authority to do the heavenly assignment that God has given them. Do you want to grow in your anointing and authority? Step out to be used by God.

It's Not in the Cards for You!

I was preaching at a church in the Monterey area of Northern California, and the pastor and his wife took me out to lunch at this nice courtyard restaurant. As we went over to the car, we walked by various shops and boutiques. I walked past a particular shop and I felt this dark rush; it was like something violently wrong was coming out of this shop.

I looked up at the sign and it was some kind of eastern New Age store. I stepped back and looked in the window. There was a black table and a woman doing tarot cards right there in front of us. Immediately, I started binding spirits and praying. I was praying but still walking away, doing the drive-by warfare thing. But I knew God was requiring something deeper from me.

We got in the car, and I knew I had unsettled business. We drove about two blocks and I began feeling sick, because I was grieving the Spirit of God. Finally I spoke up and said to the pastor, "I think I'm supposed to go back there and witness at that tarot card shop." So he turned the car back around and parked. My heart was pumping fast.

We all prayed and I walked into the shop. There were pictures on the walls of people who have headed up various "spiritual" movements in history. I felt a little Holy Ghost indignation, because they had also put Jesus' picture up there along with the other so-called ascended spiritual leaders.

I walked over and said to the tarot card reader, "Can I ask you a question?" I pointed at the cards and asked, "How do these cards help you get in touch with the spirit realm?" She said, "Would you like a reading?" I responded, "No, I would just like an answer." She said, "Give me about ten minutes," because she still needed to finish a reading with someone she was already with.

It was totally God, because had she spoken with me then, I would have tersely rebuked her, but that wasn't what the Lord had for her. The Spirit wasn't leading my attitude at that moment; I was being led by the pattern of what I've done in the past. Many times the Lord would have me confront the error, so I was in my rebuke mode.

In the next ten minutes I received a spiritual download. The Lord broke in and said, "These are the three things that you're going to say to this woman: (1) She was in a relationship with a man who she thought was going to nurture her. She trusted him and he ended up abusing her. She was then thrust out of that and got involved with the tarot cards. (2) Reading tarot cards is not what she really wants to do. She's doing this as a default. There is really a dream in her heart to do something else. Tell her that if she'll let go of this, I'll open the door for that dream. (3) I've been dealing with her. You're going to be a sign to her, and she will recognize you as such."

By then I was definitely out of my rebuke mode. I had mercy on her as I realized she had been really hurt. So I asked her the question again, "How do these cards get you in touch with the spirit realm?" She replied, "The universal wisdom of the ages that is eternal, and these cards help you to channel your energy into the cards. The sequence of cards tells a story on the basis that we can predict the future."

I couldn't help but think to myself, "And folks really buy into this? And they don't think that God can save you, or lead you, or direct you by the Word of God, or by His Spirit?"

Then the woman flipped the devil card on me. It was on now! I said to her, "You think these cards get you in touch with the spirit realm, but let me tell you about the One who got me in touch—His name is Jesus Christ. I believe that there are only two doors into the spirit realm. One is the door of darkness, and the other door is Jesus Christ."

I proceeded, "The Lord told me that you were in a relationship with a man whom you trusted, and he deeply hurt you. You thought that he would nurture you, but instead he ended up abusing you and that's how you ended up here doing tarot card readings."

I went on, "Number two, this thing that you're doing right here," I was pointing at the black table with the tarot cards, "this is not really what is in your heart to do. You've always had it in your heart to do something else, but God says, 'If you let go of this, you will have the opportunity to grab onto something else that you've desired.' Number three, God sent me back to this store as a sign to you."

By this time, she was crying and told me, "I was asking God today if He would give me a sign about whether or not I should stay involved in tarot cards." She continued, "I've always wanted to paint, but I never thought I could pay the bills by painting, so I've gotten into tarot cards. I have been contemplating if I should let go of this dream or not."

That wasn't all. She said she had grown up in a certain, ultrareligious setting, and it wasn't a good situation for her. Later on, she moved in with a guy who was a highly enlightened guru. She ended up getting hurt and abused. So I then asked, "Would it be okay if I prayed with you?"

I ended up praying with her right there on the spot, and I turned that devil card right back over. The devil was not going to whip out the last card—God was in control and He has given us His authority!

I don't think that we've even begun to tap into the authority that God has made available for us. I don't think that we've even scratched the surface of our authority as believers. For the most part we've operated in our own strength.

PROTOTYPES AND STEREOTYPES

The definition of "prototype" is an original model on which something is then patterned. In production, before anything is released for public consumerism, a prototype must be made prior to mass production. Christ's ministry is our prototype to be reproduced in us.

Jesus said, "The works that I do, he will do also; and greater works than these he will do, because I go to the Father" (John 14:12). Authority in the Bible usually means a person's right to do certain things because of the position that he or she holds. The Bible says, "But as many as received Him [Jesus Christ], to them He gave the right to become children of God" (John 1:12).

You have a position. Authority gives us the ability to use the power that God has given us because of our position with Him. God-given power can only work with God-given authority. Sometimes we feel powerless, or we become stuck in cultural, religious stereotypes. Prototypes have the power to demolish stereotypes. It's not that we're powerless; it's that we're not functioning in something that God has authorized. The power of God only flows where the authority of God has been released.

GROWING IN SPIRITUAL AUTHORITY

One day Jesus was speaking to a crowd of compelled listeners (see Mark 1:22). After He had spoken, the Word says, "And they were astonished at His teaching, for He taught them as one having authority, and not as the scribes." How do you know if someone speaks and they carry authority? For me, it's as if their words carry weight; their words are almost irresistible.

Jesus is the Son of God, but He is also the Son of Man. He is a prototype. Jesus was then not walking in the power of the Second Person of the Trinity. He was walking in what you and I have available to us. He was walking in the power of the Third Person of the Trinity, the Holy Spirit. I'm convinced that fulfilling your call on this earth requires that you continue to grow in this thing called spiritual authority. So how do we grow in spiritual authority?

Spiritual authority grows within the person who faithfully confronts the oppression threatening those on their watch. Spiritual authority increases in those who are willing to take action. In Second Corinthians 10:13-14, Paul said he had authority within the limits of a sphere, because he brought the gospel and cared for the Corinthians.

If you want to have authority in a place, it begins with you praying for those people and then sharing the gospel with them. The moment I come into a place and start sharing the gospel, authority shifts, because the gospel authenticates what the kingdom is all about.

AUTHORITY AND RESPONSIBILITY

But David said to Saul, "Your servant used to keep his father's sheep, and when a lion or a bear came and took a lamb out of the flock, I went out after it and struck it, and delivered the lamb from its mouth; and when it arose against me, I caught it by its beard, and struck and killed it. Your servant has killed both lion and bear; and this uncircumcised Philistine will be like one of them, seeing he has defied the armies of the living God." Moreover David said, "The Lord, who delivered me from the paw of the lion and from the paw of the bear, He will deliver me from the hand of this Philistine." And Saul said to David, "Go, and the Lord be with you!" (1 Samuel 17:34-37)

David had seen his brothers and the whole army of Israel run off the battlefield because Goliath came out on the field and threatened them. David came up to Saul and said, "Hey, King Saul, give me a shot. Let me fight this giant. He is saying stuff against God and that's not right. We shouldn't be running from this guy, let me fight him."

Saul said, "I can't let you go out there and fight this man, you're a youth, and he's a man of war." In other words, he was saying, "You're not ready for this; you don't have the authority, the power, or the enabling necessary to deal with this guy."

Here's David's response to this rejection from Saul, "One day I was out watching sheep. They weren't my sheep, but they were my dad's sheep. But he had entrusted me with the sheep. One day I was watching these sheep and this lion came to take out my sheep."

At that point, David had several options: (1) He could have pretended that he didn't see the sheep about to be taken. (2) He could have ran because his life was more important than the sheep's. Or, (3) He could put his life on the line because they were his dad's sheep and he wanted to protect the stewardship that had been entrusted to him. That is what he did—he fought the lion and won.

David continued talking with King Saul, "Another time I was out watching the sheep, and a bear came out." He had those same options, but he fought and took on the bear. Now he looked at King Saul and said, "I defeated the lion, I defeated the bear, and Goliath will be as one of these." You know what Saul did? He said, "Okay, but take my armor." Saul gave him the armor, because he recognized something.

The early years of David tell us something. Authority grew in David and he justified his case to allow him to go out and fight a giant, because when something that he was entrusted with was threatened, he confronted the evil that threatened it.

The opposite dynamic is also true. One day Queen Esther's uncle came to her and said, "You've been raised up for such a time as this." He said, "If you remain quiet, relief will come from somewhere else. But you and your daddy's house will perish."

Uncle Mordecai was saying, "God has given you spiritual authority, but if you remain silent while your people are perishing, you will diminish and perish in that authority. Someone else will be given that authority and they will do something with it. Not only will you perish, but wherever you do have authority, it will suffer because you didn't use what God gave you."

The way that we grow in spiritual authority is when we see someone lost or oppressed and we speak life to him or her. We prayerfully go the distance and take on the assignment that God gives us. I've seen churches shrivel in the authority God gave them for a city, because they turned deaf ears to the needs around them. Conversely, I've seen churches' "lamp stands" grow over a city because they contended and cared for the people.

Let's go back to the scribes and Jesus. Jesus rebuked them one day and gave us insight. He said to them, "You put burdens on folks that you're not even willing to move with a finger, or lift the burden off of them" (see Matt. 23:4,13). There is the secret right there—when Jesus spoke, He had authority. The scribes' voices didn't carry weight, because they weren't willing to lift the weight off of others. We need a new voice of authority in our generation. We need, in our cities, a new voice of authority. It's only going to happen when believers speak up and do what God has called them to do.

Abstaining from action in the face of danger only prolongs the wilderness. I believe there are churches that can break out of their wilderness and they don't even realize it. God loves you too much to let you out of that season without depositing in you what He wants. But there are others who are in wildernesses because they've abstained from action when God said to do something.

If you could see in the spirit realm, you would see your authority enlarge when you step out. When we evangelize and break oppression off of people, we rise to new levels in spiritual authority. I believe the same is true with praying for the sick. How did I begin to pray for the sick and start seeing results? I just prayed for a lot of sick people. If you want to grow in authority and have greater effectiveness praying for the sick, start praying and don't worry about results. You just trust God and pray, and don't stop just because you don't see anything. It's a process of taking on a lion and a bear, so you can be trusted with a Goliath kind of healing. Soul winning follows the same lines.

We carry the light of Christ and we mustn't fail to recognize the exciting spiritual impact we have on the world before us, as well as the darkness around us. Let's step into the dunamis lifestyle.

CHAPTER 12

THE JESUS STYLE

PUTTING IT ALL TOGETHER, the consummate prophetic evangelist is Jesus Christ. No one has ever given as much and has been so passionate for souls. Christ reveals each dimension that has been described in the pages of this book.

Watching Him move through the Gospels has always been an incredible thrill for me. The Bible refers to Him as "the captain of our salvation" (Heb. 2:10). This term means "the author" and "one that takes the lead in anything." Even as John the Revelator described the great innumerable multitude in Heaven, amongst the festivities there was a collective cry of, "Salvation belongs to our God." After which, everybody falls on their "celestial" faces. The Lamb is not only the originator but the proprietor of this incredible dynamic called salvation.

In the culmination of human history there is a dawning understanding that Jesus encompasses and emanates the essence of redemption. He is both the mastermind and the masterpiece of the spiritual reclamation of souls.

Then Jesus said to them, "Follow Me, and I will make you become fishers of men" (Mark 1:17).

If you're following Jesus, you should be catching fish. God is going to cause you to be an attractive magnet, a Holy Ghost fishing net, to see the fish come in. He will work on you to become a prophetic evangelist. You don't have to get there on your own. Jesus said, "Follow Me." In other words, "I'm setting the example, so follow My example." Jesus' desire is that His life would be reproduced in us, that we would model our ministry after Him. That is why I call this chapter "The Jesus Style."

Then Jesus answered and said to them, "Most assuredly, I say to you, the Son can do nothing of Himself, but what He sees the Father do; for whatever He does, the Son also does in like manner. For the Father loves the Son, and shows Him all things that He Himself does; and He will show Him greater works than these, that you may marvel" (John 5:19-20).

Prophetic evangelism is seeing God doing something, and then joining Him.

We can do nothing of ourselves, but that's not the end of the Scripture! "What He sees the Father do, the Son can do." Here's the key: If I can see the Father doing it, I can do it. If you can see God do it, you can put your hand to it and partner with Him. The key is the ability to see what He's doing. Let's take it a step further. If you are seeing something that God is doing, it is an invitation for your participation. If you can see it, you can do it. Since God loves us, He shows us all things. Stand on that before you go witnessing to someone.

The word used for "shows" means "exposed to the eyes, to exhibit, to make known." You can pray when you go to evangelize, "God, I thank You in advance that You're going to expose people's fault lines to my eyes."

Because the Father loves us, He promises to reveal to us what He's doing so we can partner with Him. The Son did nothing apart from what the Father showed Him. God wants to move in a church service or in a divine appointment more than you do. Daily, I ask the Lord to show me something that will happen during my day, and He is always faithful to show me something. If you feed on this revelation you will have something released in you that will change everything around you.

DROPPING SOME KNOWLEDGE

But the Helper, the Holy Spirit, whom the Father will send in My name, He will teach you all things, and bring to your remembrance all things that I said to you (John 14:26).

This phrase "all things" is important and means there is nothing that He leaves out. The words "bring to remembrance" means to put in mind. So when the Holy Spirit says, "I'm going to bring to your remembrance," what it means is the Holy Spirit is going to put something into your mind. This is prophetic evangelism. When you're witnessing to someone, the Holy Spirit is going to put into your mind what you need to say—supernatural downloading.

The woman with the issue of blood said to herself, "If I could just touch the hem of Jesus' garment I will be made whole." Where did that come from? It was put into her mind by the Holy Spirit. It was God directing her.

For "who has known the mind of the Lord that he may instruct Him?" But we have the mind of Christ (1 Corinthians 2:16).

Thank God that we have the mind of Christ! You just have to access it. Maybe one of the greatest gifts to have in this hour, outside of the Spirit of Christ, is the mind of Christ. We must possess the mind of Christ because without it:

1. Witnessing tends to get off track. I've found that if I don't have the mind of Christ, I tend to get off onto bunny trails.

2. We tend to pander to people's fleshly desires.

In other words, if I don't have the mind of Christ, I'm always going to go toward what they want. There is an aspect where you address their needs, but we've got to go deeper to their spiritual need, rather than their fleshly desires. Jesus rebuked Peter and said, "Get behind Me satan. You have your mind on things of man, not the things of God."

3. We miss hitting people's spiritual needs.

TWELVE PRINCIPLES OF JESUS' STYLE OF HARVESTING FROM JOHN 4

Principle 1—Break the holding pattern.

Overcoming the inertia of stagnation and breaking the sound barrier of communication is so significant.

Introductory moments are crucial to the overall flow of witnessing; sometimes just stepping out will release God into a situation. Jesus initiated the conversation with the Samaritan woman.

One of the keys to breaking the holding pattern is to be clear regarding your purpose. We must also get others out of holding patterns. Turning objections into opportunities can release people from a spiritual stalemate. Jesus found a "window" and utilized the "latch" of a word of knowledge. The trigger element was revelation. Revelation is an ongoing participation in the life of Christ.

Principle 2—Sense the where or the what, before the who.

John 4:4 says, "But He needed to go through Samaria." Why did Jesus need to go through Samaria?

The word *needed* means to "bind, fasten under chains, put under obligation." Have you ever felt that you were drawn to a place and it seemed like you were obligated to go there and you didn't know why?

A woman of Samaria came to draw water. Jesus said to her, "Give Me a drink" (John 4:7).

Jesus was there before the woman got there. Prophetic evangelism will draw you to places before the people even get there—that's prophetic. Evangelists can be drawn to a person once he sees them, but prophetic evangelists can be drawn to a spot before the person even gets there.

I believe that Jesus saw the woman when she came to the well and He knew she was the one. She was the reason He had been led to the well. The disciples went to get food, but Jesus didn't go with them. Witnessing can begin by being drawn to people, a burden coupled with an intense excitement. This is how it registers for me. I'm drawn to a person and I get excited that I'm drawn to them as if I know they're going to get saved. As you're being drawn to people, you may not realize it, but they are also being drawn to the God in you. You don't always make the connection, but it's happening in the Spirit. I call it "the attraction gift." If you are drawn to them, believe that they will be drawn to you.

People can sense it when you go into a witnessing situation and you're not confident, there's a different atmosphere due to your awkward disposition. But if you know that God has told you to speak to that person, you can go into the situation with faith and confidence.

Principle 3—Begin where people "are."

Jesus said to the woman at the well, "Give me a drink." The woman was an expert in H_2O. Every day she was at the well drawing water. Make your point of contact between the gospel and the person's specific need; find out what they care about. This woman obviously cared about water. (She also cared about men.)

Jesus entered her world and her arena. If we're going to be prophetic evangelists we can't be cocooning. We tend to believe that we'll be defiled if we go into a particular place. Now understand that you can't take this to an extreme; you've got to use wisdom, get God's direction, and be armed with the Holy Spirit to enter into their arena.

Speak in the language of the person or people. Don't come out there with all of this "Christian-ese" that the world doesn't even understand. Begin to learn how to communicate the gospel message, and your testimony, in ways that are relevant to the culture today. (For example, don't say, "Let me give you my testimony." Say instead, "Let me tell you my story.") Prophets always spoke in the language of the culture of the day. Be ready to discern the entry places in people's lives. This well of water was the entry point in this woman's life.

Then the woman of Samaria said to Him, "How is it that You, being a Jew, ask a drink from me, a Samaritan woman?" For Jews have no dealings with Samaritans (John 4:9).

This was a moment that hit the proverbial wall. But when you're a prophetic evangelist, and you hit a wall, just keep on engaging because God is going to give you a window. If they are not walking away, there must be a reason that they are still listening to you.

Jesus kept going and found a window. That's faith; He was finding the entry point. It's interesting to note that Jesus didn't even address their racial or sexual differences. She spoke her objection and His only reply was, "If you knew the Gift, you would say to Me, 'Give me a drink,' and then you would have living water inside of you."

Principle 4—"Can" the canned techniques.

If God directs you to use a rehearsed technique, go for it, but if your mentality is stuck on that same technique over and over again, something needs to change. People with mechanical mind-sets tend to jump to conclusions. They see a problem and they immediately decide on what they think is the solution. You've got to be able to keep your adversary on the back of his heels not knowing what you're going to do. People are different; Jesus never did the same thing every single time.

He did different things in different situations, even when it came to healing.

Jesus just implemented what He was discerning and sensing. What you sense, you say. Be free to do that! What you perceive, you put in practice. As you're witnessing to someone, all of a sudden you're sensing that they don't have a good relationship with their dad. Just begin to speak and ask questions about that issue. Talk about your relationship with your dad and your heavenly Father being your dad. Or you can use the example of a friend. You need to trust that sensing.

Realize that the Holy Spirit is working on a person to receive as much as He is working on you to share. Watch the things you perceive as you're witnessing to people. This is how the prophetic injects into your evangelism. If I'm conversing with someone and I sense that I hit a certain aspect of witnessing where they become distant, what I do is keep talking and say something like, "I don't know what it is, just now when I was talking it feels like the temperature just dropped ten degrees in here. What did I say that caused you to do that?" You can address it right there.

Typically, we pretend we don't sense it, but the reason why we're picking up on it is because we need to address that thing. We're afraid of being confrontational, but it just depends how you approach it. Be honest, and people will be honest with you.

> But when they deliver you up, do not worry about how or what you should speak. For it will be given to you in that hour what you should speak; for it is not you who speak, but the Spirit of your Father who speaks in you (Matthew 10:19-20).

You never have to prepare your exact words beforehand. On the other hand, the Bible also says to show yourself approved. You need to be ready to give a defense, but you need to have a balance. We study the Word so that the Holy Spirit can bring all things to our remembrance. But what He's saying is that you can trust that the Father is going to speak inside of you. I can go into a witnessing situation with confidence because I know that the Father is going to speak through me. God is going to give you something to say! He cares about the lost way too much to leave them that way. God isn't sending you out there to fail; He's sending you out to be effective in harvesting.

Principle 5—Trust the anointing that is on you.

First John 2:27 says, in essence, "You have an anointing inside of you and it teaches you; it's true and not a lie."

Why would John say this anointing that is on you is true? Why should you believe what you are sensing you should say is really God speaking through you? What if it's not God? In the process of stepping out, you're going to find out what is and what is not God. You will never know by playing it safe.

Solid food belongs to those who are mature, who by reason and use, have their senses trained to discern good and evil (see Heb. 5:14). When your heart is right and you're prayed up, that anointing is going to be on you. The Bible says that the anointing teaches you, it instructs you, it leads you, and it is true and not a lie.

Capitalize on those things that you sense in your heart and use them as the Spirit leads. Prophetic evangelism is a walk of listening to the Anointed One who lives inside of you. It is getting to the place Jesus was when He trusted the anointing that was inside of Him. Even though the disciples were going to go out and get food, Jesus felt the need to stop off at this well in Samaria, even though He may not have known why. Just as we do, He had to trust the leading of the Holy Spirit.

We tend to think that everything came to Jesus in a clear, audible voice from the Father. No, it might have just been a light impression. If He wasn't looking for it, He could have missed it.

Principle 6—Cultivate spiritual curiosity in others.

The woman said to Him, "Sir, You have nothing to draw with, and the well is deep. Where then do You get that living water?" (John 4:11)

He was able to get her to ask the questions. God is going to get you to a place where people are going to ask you questions about spiritual reality. You will be able to cultivate spiritual curiosity in others.

It's interesting that Jesus happened to go to a well that had significance for her. It wasn't just any well, it was the well that she went to. She asked, "Are you greater than our Father Jacob who gave us the well and drank from it?" Jesus again didn't answer that question. He didn't explain how much greater He was.

He stayed on focus and said, "Whoever drinks of this well will thirst again." In essence, He was saying that everything you've tried has left you with an unanswered dimension in your heart. You have tried to do many things to appease that cry, but it still goes unanswered. I could give you something right now where you would find substance, fulfillment, and release of the things that you have desired." The woman then said that she wanted it.

Sowing Into the Divine Function

Witnessing or engaging non-Christians in productive conversation is an art. We've already talked about the prophetic aspect of God releasing, but there's another aspect. Witnessing requires the constant development of skill, studying, along with nurturing, by prayer and openness to the Holy Spirit. You become better at witnessing by witnessing. That's what I mean by an art. An art is something that you practice and continually work at to become better and better.

We must have spiritual sensitivity, which requires us to put up our spiritual antennas. When you're engaging a non-Christian in productive conversation, look for trigger moments and trigger places. Anytime a person expresses their wound or hurt to me, or they become vulnerable to me in conversation, it speaks volumes to me. Maybe someone else would pass by it, but for me it is as if I struck gold. It's a trigger moment. Listen for trigger phrases: problems in their family or in their relationships. There needs to be a contrast between presenting the facts versus cultivating someone's heart. Jesus was an expert at cultivating people's hearts. The Bible says that common people loved to listen to Him.

Even an adulteress, caught in the act, felt safe around Jesus.

The bottom line is that a sinner is going to sin. The only sin that you're dealing with in that moment is the sin of not receiving Jesus Christ. You don't clean fish before you catch them; you catch them and then you clean them.

Principle 7—Know when to hold up, know when to fold up.

Jesus never forced Himself on anyone. If they didn't want to hear it, He didn't force it. Jesus rebuked some Pharisees, but if people didn't want to hear, the Bible says, "He knew what was in their hearts and did not disclose Himself to them." Pray that God would continually cultivate their hearts, but don't try to force the tilling of their fallow ground on them.

Recognize when people respond positively to a conversation about spirituality. Look for receptivity in others. I call it testing the waters. When you're with some people, test the waters by throwing something out there to see how they'll respond to it.

Receptivity in others can be seen in their:

1. **Willingness to engage.** Are they open to a conversation with you? I sit next to people on planes and if they have a willingness to engage in conversation, I'll begin to witness to them.

2. **Interest in spirituality.** Some Christians are intimidated by people who talk about their horoscopes, demonic movies, or the psychics they've called, but I think it's a great opportunity. This tells me that there is obviously a spiritual search going on.

   The modernistic viewpoint says, "It's all about secularism. Man is the answer to his own dilemma." Postmodernism has leveled the playing field and says anything is right. Some people think that this makes it more of a challenge, but I'd rather deal with that than deal with the smug modernist. The postmodernists say they're open to anything. Maybe they're too open, but at least it opens the door for the right One to come in.

3. **Openness to hear about personal experiences.** You can say to someone, "Hey, can I tell you about something that just happened to me?" If they're open to hearing about your personal experience, begin to share a testimony, or someone else's testimony. I typically ask them about "their story." I ask them about themselves and what they do, their family life, and listen for a while. Soon the conversation will come back to me and they ask what I do.

Since I have been sitting there spending about 20 minutes letting them go on and on about their stock options and everything else, it clearly becomes my turn to tell them that I'm a minister. They normally say something like, "Oh, really. So what is that?" So I then share the whole thing. There is now receptivity. If you sow the gift of listening to others, they will sow it back to you even if it's out of obligation.

We've got to know when to talk, and we need to know when to walk. Believe it or not, there's a time to walk. You need to know when it is a good point to leave the subject of spiritual things, when they've hit their brakes.

Our most effective evangelistic opportunities are simply obedient responses to the Father's invitation to enter into a situation where the Holy Spirit is already working. Jesus only did that which He saw the Father do.

There is a Christian mind-set that says you need to be witnessing to everybody, all the time. I used to be under that thing. I was frequently under condemnation: "Oh, I'm not witnessing enough," and I would really get down on myself. If the Holy Spirit isn't in it, you don't want to be in it.

Principle 8—Keep the conversation on focus.

One of the things that you've got to be aware of is the atmosphere, and predominate cultural climate.

Don't let the conversation go off onto futile bunny trails. Keep bringing it back to Jesus. Jesus could have been detoured with the woman at the well. He could have gotten onto the racial topic or whether He was greater than the person who built the well. Jesus kept the conversation on track.

In every generation there's a dominant climate of opinion, so be aware, and be ready to handle that. Be ready for some of the arguments that are going to come. Without the Holy Spirit helping you tackle objections, your words are going to be futile. I try not to ever get into an argument. I'm not trying to win an argument; I'm trying to win a person. In tense situations, I might say something like, "All arguments aside, all I know is that Jesus Christ saved my life." People aren't going to argue with your personal testimony.

Principle 9—Put their ears back on.

Sometimes you've got to earn the right to be heard. Sometimes you've got to clean up some other Christians' messes. This is what I call "janitorial" evangelism. Sometimes the last person or the last church service that witnessed to that person had some sort of dysfunction and it left a mess.

The woman at the well said, "Our fathers worship in the mountains, you Jews say that Jerusalem is the place where we ought to worship." Obviously there had been some conflict and Jesus was ready to clean up the messes.

In Luke 22:50, there was a servant of the High Priest named Malchus, who came to apprehend Jesus for His trial and crucifixion. Peter pulled out his sword and cut off his ear. Jesus picked it up and put it back on his head—completely healed. Just as Jesus put Malchus's ear back on, the challenge for prophetic evangelists is to put people's ears back on in this lost generation. We need to do what we have to do to gain a hearing and a respect for our message.

Every time I stand up in the open air on college campuses I'm thinking, "They've lost their ears. What can I say? Holy Spirit, give me something to say that will put their ears back on." When people don't have ears to hear, what you communicate to them will end in misunderstanding and resistance. Whenever you run into a lot of resistance and misunderstanding, stop and recognize that your hearers' ears aren't on. Begin to pray that God would do what He needs to do to get their ears working right.

Principle 10—Do justice; love mercy.

Jesus gave the woman at the well a word of knowledge.

One of the definitions of a *word of knowledge* is "a supernatural insight, revealed by the Holy Spirit, that gives a believer specific information about a person spontaneously." A prophetic word from the Holy Spirit can instantly turn people from a negative to a positive view of God.

Jesus said to this woman, "Go call your husband." Notice that He didn't begin with saying, "I know that you're living with a dude who you're not married to and you're a five time divorcee."

She said, "I have no husband." He said, "You have rightly said that you have no husband." He didn't harp on her living with a guy and having five husbands. He didn't even come back and address that issue again. It was like He just let her know that He knew that about her. He then began to address the wound in her that had led her to the sin. The wound was that she had a heart to worship, but her adoration had been placed on men. From that point on Jesus just challenged her to place her adoration on God.

Jesus never humiliated people. He always maintained the dignity of the lost when He addressed them. He confronted the religious Pharisees, but He never exposed lost people.

The great minister, R.A. Torrey, in his rules about witnessing, said, "Never embarrass the person." I've seen guys come onto the college campus and embarrass the students who are lost. This almost always places further hindrances in their minds to block them from understanding God's love for them.

When Jesus caught a woman in adultery, He didn't make a judgmental comment to her. When a prostitute was washing Jesus' feet, He didn't say, "Get away from me, you disgusting woman!" Jesus always left the lost with their dignity. It was Jesus' style.

The Word of God tells us to do justice and love mercy. It does not say to love justice and do mercy, there's a big difference in so many people's interpretation of this. As representatives of the good news of the gospel, we must sow mercy into wounded, sinful lives. This is hard sometimes because we have the mistaken idea that if we don't call out their sin, they won't be aware of their need for God.

I understand that there are some extremely hard people today who may need to be shocked into realizing what they are actually doing, but for the most part this postmodern generation doesn't necessarily need their sin pointed out. Instead, we will more effectively point them to their Answer and their Healer by pointing out their wounds, their hurts, and their aches.

After her loving experience with Jesus, that woman at the well got saved, walked back to her city, told them all about her experience, and the whole city went out and heard Jesus themselves and decided to believe too! An entire citywide awakening happened because Jesus had a prophetic evangelistic moment at a well! Jesus never treated people as the enemy; He knew the real enemy. If you're going to be a prophetic evangelist, always remember who is the real enemy. Don't get angry at the person—love the person.

Principle 11—Recognize that conviction is a divine process.

I call it "the organic versus the inorganic." Soul winning is organic; it's more of a process than an event.

Something organic is something that grows; it is derived from a living organism and developed over a process of time. We need to take the time to groom relationships with people.

There are four stages of organic soul winning:

1. Cultivating—Building a relationship and establishing a rapport with the unchurched.
2. Planting—Post-introductory breakthroughs with the gospel message.
3. Nurturing—Utilizing a relational platform to expand one's knowledge base of the gospel.
4. Harvesting—Bringing a person to a salvation decision through love and friendship.

There are times where just getting a prophetic word is not what it's going to take to open up a broken heart; it's going to require taking the time to build a relationship. What we do have today is a lot of inorganic witnessing. Inorganic means not growing from something natural, but coming from something that is unnatural. We do too many inorganic methods of evangelism. If it is impersonal or insensitive, chances are the method is inorganic. The postmodern generation is infatuated with organic things. We must take this fact into consideration and go out of our way to build redemptive relationships with people.

You know what Jesus likened the kingdom of God to? He likened the kingdom of God to a man who planted a seed in the ground and went to sleep. He didn't know how it happened, but the seed grew, first the blade, then the head, then the full grain. Jesus was describing the kingdom of God as an organic process.

When you're witnessing to someone, the ability to sense ripeness is crucial. Sometimes, even though I want to say, "Let's pray," I know that it would be premature, because we have not yet come to that place where it's ripe. The revelation of what God wants to do in a person has not fully dawned on them, so it's better to wait. Other times I absolutely know it's time to pray. Ask God for the ability to sense the ripeness in people. You may not even have a deep relationship with someone, but you might be standing next to them when your "ripeness meter" goes off! The Holy Spirit will direct and cause you to know the conditions of those He sends you to.

What kind of person do I need to be to make the gospel attractive to this audience or individual? Paul said this, "I have become all things to all men, that I might by all means save some" (1 Cor. 9:22). We need to ask ourselves, "What do I need to do to make the gospel attractive without compromising?" Relate to them where they are, all the while listening to the Holy Spirit's guidance. If you do this as the Spirit leads, you're going to find open doors.

Evangelism is not something we do to people; it's something we do with the gospel. The Good News is something we share. Just living your life in a way that attracts people to Jesus in you is the starting block of sharing the gospel; I'm still evangelizing when I'm doing that. Your life becomes a classroom for the next generation and people are going to learn from you.

Principle 12—Recapture the narrative and retell the story.

We must realize that the gospel is essentially a riveting, engaging, real-life story. The devil wants to keep you from realizing that your part of this story matters. Your testimony of what the gospel has done in your life is real because first-person witnessing is always the most effective. This is an authentic perception in today's culture. We must overcome our concept of our "private" faith and open up our lives in as transparent a manner as we can. It's important to be transparent and vulnerable. When people hear a voice with a story that they can relate to, they are open to believing what they are hearing.

The city of Samaria was moved by the woman's first-person testimony and many believed and conversions resulted. I'm convinced that as we follow in Jesus' example we can be assured that consistent fruit and miracle harvests will result. God wants to bless you with lasting impacting conversions.

The end result of the Jesus style is that woman getting saved, and her entire city along with her. Who could have known that one woman, of some disrepute, would come back from a firsthand experience with the Living gospel Himself and have that kind of influence where an entire city would walk out of their way to go hear a new spiritual leader? The Jesus Style gives us the ultimate modeling for prophetic evangelism!

THE ART OF GIVING
EVANGELISTIC APPEALS

IN THIS SECTION OF THE BOOK, I am going to share principles from my life that I believe will help you become much more effective in giving an evangelistic appeal.

I've preached the gospel in a variety of places including street corners and campuses. These principles will help if you're doing one-on-one witnessing, but they will especially help when you get an opportunity to stand before people at your work, in your classroom, and when you go open-air on the streets.

Revivalist George Whitefield is one of my favorite people in Church history. When a man was to be hung, he used to stand up on the gallows and preach on Hebrews 9:27, "And as it is appointed for men to die once, but after this the judgment." He seized the moment to give an evangelistic appeal because folks had just seen some dude up there on the gallows go into the eternal realm.

George Whitefield once said, "I preach as a dying man to a dying world." I believe that we could learn so much from him on how to win people to the Lord. One of the main reasons why people don't accept Christ is because the appeal is off. We have not appealed to people "rightly."

Let me define *appeal*. Webster's dictionary tells us that an appeal is:

223

1. "A legal proceeding by which a case is brought before a higher court for review of the decision of a lower court."

When we're calling people, we are making an appeal to them. The earthly court of opinions says that God is just another cosmic head on the ledge with all of the other religious leaders in the world. But we're coming from a higher court.

2. "The power of arousing a sympathetic response."

Author Terry Crist is right when he says that, "One of the symptoms of being religious isolationists is that you have lost much of the ability to communicate naturally." We must regain appeal. We ought to be salt in the capacity that we make people thirsty by our communication.

We've lost that—the worst thing you could do when a person is wounded is to pour salt into their wound. I've witnessed self-righteous ministers do this. They don't know their audience.

3. "Attractiveness that interests, pleases, or stimulates."

I want to share the gospel in a way that is attractive, that sparks interest, pleases, and stimulates. I want to speak to that God deposit inside of people. Ecclesiastes 3:11 says, "He has put eternity in their hearts." There is something already going on in people's hearts.

I want to look around and find traces of what God is doing. If you are going to be what I call a postmodern prophetic evangelist, you've got to be a person with these three things:

1. You have to be a person of fire. You have got to have the fire of God in you! The spirit of the gospel must burn like fire in you or it will be quenched by the spirit of this age.

The moment you get into the intellectual wrangling, you will lose the fire. Go for the fire! Our mouths proclaim the gospel but our hearts are where the spirit of the gospel must burn. So you have got to have fire in your heart.

If you're going to give an evangelistic appeal, you have got to recognize the appeal begins with your own life. They say there are two reasons why people don't come to church: (A) They don't know a Christian, or (B) They do know a Christian. Ouch!

2. You have to be a person with vision. If you're going to be a prophetic postmodern evangelist, you have to be a person of vision.

Vision is like a confident pilot in his airplane, flying through a storm. When you've got vision, you can handle the storms. Vision is what causes one to step up and endure what it takes to become effective. If you don't have vision in witnessing, you are going to give up on folks. If you lead one person to Christ, you're addicted for life.

3. You have to be a person of communication. A great communicator can turn an ear into an eye. If you're going to be great at giving evangelistic appeals, you've got to know your audience.

Don't make the mistake of assuming that everybody is like you. The problem with that assumption is you will only win people to the Lord who are like you. Communication is less about information and more about identification. Paul became "all things to all people" so that he could win them to Christ.

Paul presented the gospel to the philosophers on Mars Hill who were the most culturally sensitive, materialistic, new-aged, unreached target group in history. Yet he walked away with folks who got saved. Here's what I would recommend for an evangelistic appeal:

Find the playing field of meaningful dialog and debate. What is meaningful to the people who you're trying to speak to? You have to start where people are at. We need to bridge the gap with natural talk without feeling like we're unspiritual.

Styles of Delivery:

1. Jehu's style (see 2 Kings 10:11): Jehu, had a battering ram sledgehammer, and he destroyed Baal out of Israel.

2. Paul's style (see Acts 17:16-34): You can displace the false by the introduction of the truth. Paul was a stealth bomber carrying smart bombs.

One of the most outstanding characteristics of Jesus' ministry is His ability to communicate with common folks. The Bible says that the common people used to love listening to Him. Utilize the power of shared beliefs. A Japanese manufacturer was asked, "What's the best language to do business in?" The Japanese manufacturer's response was, "My customer's language."

Let me share some cultural characteristics:

A. Culture is the unspoken communication of society; it speaks without being audible. Culture is language. If we don't take that into consideration then we're not speaking in light of understanding. Jesus referred to people's workplaces, their homes, and their farms. He was aware of their culture.

B.   Culture is the operating system of the mind. People operate in autopilot; they don't even realize why they do what they do, because their culture is downloaded every day.

C.   Culture is the avenue for God's revelation. God chose to send Jesus into culture as a man, in fact, a man everyone could relate to. The term is incarnated.

D.   All churches are culturally relevant. Some are simply relevant with a different culture. They may be relevant with a culture of people from 1933 and may not be relevant to the current hour.

The following are ways that I have seen people come to Christ:

1. An awareness of insufficiency. Somewhere along the line, people became aware that something is missing in their lives. They become aware of a need, a sense of unrest, and they come to Christ.

2. The registering of eternal desires. People look at their lives and think, "There's got to be more." They may have the money, the lovers, and the popularity, but it's all vanity. People get saved because all of a sudden they want something beyond what they have.

3. An appreciation of the God-factor. People come to Christ because they recognize that Christ has a gift to give and it hits them. Maybe it's love, maybe it's mercy, maybe it's peace of mind, but it's something they know can only come from God. Sometimes people understand how sin pays off. Sin is a taskmaster that pays off in death, and their eyes are opened and they see that sin hollows them out.

4. An "epiphany moment." It's when Heaven invades your world big time! I had one of those experiences when I got saved. It's when something supernatural, transcendent, something that's almost considered paranormal, enters your world.

A TOUGH CROWD

Paul dealt with the self-righteous folks and the Jews, all in this passage in Acts 17. He dealt with the carnality of Epicureans, and the indifference of the Stoics. Those are some tough audiences. Paul argues that stoic pantheism and epicurean deism both contain elements of truth, but Christian theology provides the most adequate view of God.

Paul tackles all of them on one trip. If we're going to turn people from darkness to light, their eyes must first be opened to see the difference between darkness and light. If I'm giving an evangelistic appeal, I have to help the lost have an eye-opening experience. Begin to pray for that opening.

> ...*for as I was passing through and considering the objects of your worship, I even found an altar with this inscription: TO THE UNKNOWN GOD. Therefore, the One whom you worship without knowing, Him I proclaim to you* (Acts 17:23).

Paul walked through the streets of Athens and took in the culture. He went out in the middle of their student union. He looked and listened to conversations at the coffee shops. He hung around their office cubicles, he could hear their conversations. He took his time and simply observed.

The Bible says "he was provoked." I think that he was provoked because of the spirit of ignorance and deception that was corrupting the dignity of God's creation. I don't think that he was actually mad at the people. God created the human spirit to respond to love and expectation. If you walk around being angry with folks, you're not going to win any of them.

Tips on Marketplace Messages

You might wonder how I get a word when I preach open air. Or how do I know what to say when I share with a group, or a church? I pray until a theme attacks me, until I'm overwhelmed by what God is gripping my heart with. If it doesn't grip me, it's not going to grip them, so I need to begin with something that grips me.

So I just pray that God will give something to me. Sometimes it's a thought or a phrase. Paul didn't begin his appeal with Scripture in this situation. He began by paying them a compliment. Remember, calling someone "religious" was a compliment back in that day. He was paying a compliment to people who had idols all over the place.

It's not where we end but where we begin. If I start at the right place with an unbeliever, they're not going to be offended in the end, for the most part. It's about where we begin which is where the offense can be found.

Paul was provoked, but notice that his outrage was aimed at idolatry and darkness. When I preach open air I have two options. I could be the stealth bomber, or I can be the sledgehammer. (The stealth bomber is very effective because the target never sees it coming.)

What is the Holy Spirit dealing with this person about? We need to hear the voice of the Spirit. There have been times when even in the process of talking, I can see that I've hit on the exact thing the person has been devastated by. They perk up and start asking questions. Next thing I know, I'm leading them to the Lord.

You must envision yourself as a prophetic warning to your generation. In Acts chapter 2 there's another open-air occasion, and Peter says, "Save yourself from this perverse generation."

> *Therefore he reasoned in the synagogue with the Jews and with the Gentile worshipers, and in the marketplace daily with those who happened to be there* (Acts 17:17).

You must build relationships and build rapport. When I go as an evangelist and speak to a church, the success of the outreach is not built so much on what I say, but it is based on that church's rapport and relationship with the community before I even get there. If they've got bad relationship and a bad rapport in their community, people who don't know God won't come out to the outreach, so it dies before it even takes off.

Paul was in the marketplace daily. He wasn't just hanging out in the synagogue; he was out in the marketplace. If you're going to give an evangelistic appeal you need to be around the people. Paul was hearing their language and building relationship.

> *Now while Paul waited for them at Athens, his spirit was provoked within him when he saw that the city was given over to idols. ...Then Paul stood in the midst of the Areopagus and said, "Men of Athens, I perceive that in all things you are very religious"* (Acts 17:16,22).

Paul saw altars all over the place, but he also saw the redemptive aspect of their sin. He saw instinctive cravings in their hearts toward worship. Instead of bashing them for having idols, he looked at the redemptive cry in their heart and linked it to something that was higher than their sin. Find, in the people themselves, the beginning of your message.

FINDING RELEVANT KEYS

...for in Him we live and move and have our being, as also some of your own poets have said, "For we are also His off-spring" (Acts 17:28).

Paul was in possession of some knowledge. He quoted their poets because he actually knew secular poets. Be aware of what's going on. I've spoken open air and I've dropped one thought about a currently popular icon and everybody stopped to listen.

When Paul spoke he did not awaken their animosity as if his mission was to destroy their entire culture. It is the same with you. Your mission is to preach Christ to people and bring Him into their culture. God isn't trying to destroy the whole culture; the culture simply becomes a medium.

I've preached open air and used all kinds of openings. Once, it was the three little pigs as an analogy. I preached that you can't build your house out of straw or the big bad wolf will blow your house down, but you need to build your house on the Rock. Folks prayed with me that day and got saved! Yes, my text may have been the three little pigs, but I didn't close without giving the gospel message. Your testimony might just be your text; a current event might be your text.

In that altar Paul found a communication key that would fit into the lock of the minds and the hearts of the people. Their hearts needed to be a new altar from the true, living God. Paul answers the question,

"Is there a need for a new altar?" When you give an evangelistic appeal there is always a key. You must find that key.

Here is another thing prophetic postmodern evangelist's do; they interpret for people things they cannot interpret for themselves. For example, do you know why people listen to certain kinds of music?

Because the lyrics of the songs articulate what a generation is feeling but cannot describe.

Let's keep looking to Paul's example and how he interpreted what was going on in the people's culture.

1. Find cultural fault lines. Look for the place where there are discrepancies in the culture. We must expose secularism's troubling implications. You cannot build a foundation for a culture on something that is unknown, nor can you have virtue in your society if it's unknown. Every lost person in the world has a sign on them that says, "To an unknown god." They don't know, but we have to tell them who it is. As I preach on campuses, I find that more people are "neo-atheists" out of convenience than conviction. We must root out their reasons for unbelief.

2. Place Jesus and His salvation for people within their immediate grasp.

> *And He has made from one blood every nation of men to dwell on all the face of the earth, and has determined their preappointed times and the boundaries of their dwellings, so that they should seek the Lord, in the hope that they might grope for Him and find Him, though He is not far from each one of us* (Acts 17:26-27).

If I'm going to preach, I don't want people to feel like God is mad at them or far away from them. I tell people that it doesn't matter what they've done or how bad it's gotten for them, they are still only one decision away from the ultimate good. I tell them: "All that has to come out of your mouth right now is Jesus Christ is Lord, and at the end of that confession there is a new life for you."

3. Paul revealed the spirituality of God. In order to be an accepted communicator of truth that is yet unknown to the non-Christian, you start out by resonating what they already believe to be true. Paul specialized in this before the Athenians.

BACK IN THE DAY

Notice that in Acts 17:23, he began by saying they were religious, then he talked about the poets. He then referred to the unknown god. In 700 B.C. there was a man by the name of Epimenides that he and others considered to be a prophet (which may be a generous term for him). The following stories were recorded in the writings of the third century Greek historian, Diogenes Laertius.

It was six centuries before Christ and there was a horrible disease throughout the land. In Athens, this plague was killing people left and right. They put up many, many, altars to all different kinds of gods trying to get the gods to take the plague away.

Finally, the people called on Epimenides, a Greek philosopher and wise man. They decide to solicit his wisdom. His prescription was based on three assumptions:

1. There must be an unseen God they did not know.
2. That God was great and big enough to stop the plague.
3. This God would have mercy on them if they acknowledged their ignorance of Him.

With this assumption in mind, Epimenides decided to offer this god a sacrifice. They didn't know who that unknown god was but they appealed to the one true God, even though they didn't know Him. It is supernatural what took place. History tells us that when they made that sacrifice, the plague stopped in Athens.

Approximately 750 years later, Paul stood up and said, "Your forefathers put up this altar because a horrible plague was killing your ancestors. The stories have been passed down from generation to generation that there is this one god whom you don't know, but I've come here to tell you who that God is."

Paul continued, "God is a God who does not need someone to create Him. He is the Creator. He has overlooked ignorance in the past but now is the time, you've got to repent. The God who saved your civilization is the same God that is going to save you right now." The Bible says that right on the spot, some people gave their lives to Christ. Paul's approach was both prophetic and strategic.

Paul's arguments were met with three different responses: mocking (see Acts 17:32), interest (see Acts 17:32), and repentance (see Acts 17:34). This corresponds to Paul's threefold desire to interest, persuade, and confront. This sets up the platform to call for a response.

231

CALLING FOR A RESPONSE

Spiritual leader, Mike Bickle, told me that he believes the reason why more Christians aren't effective in leading people to Christ is that they don't know how to close the deal.

The gospel of Jesus Christ demands a decision. The invitation ought to come with urgency and straightforwardness. It's so important to believe that God is drawing people and to expect them to respond. We must call for a response out of the conviction that we are authorized by God even if no one responds, and set the atmosphere for future decisions.

Evangelist Leighton Ford says, "An evangelistic message ought to move on a constantly ascending line as it comes to its climax, and a high moment ought to come when the preacher finishes his appeal."

Many times as I am giving an altar call I'll describe the fears, inner longings, hesitations, and questions of those who are deliberating on this monumental decision. My goal is to help people get in touch with their emptiness and longings. My other goal is to compassionately confront the myths and put the brakes on any delusions. I want the seeker to feel like the most insane and hopeless thing they could do is to stay lost.

Billy Graham states rightly that, "Conversion is definitely more than a psychological phenomenon—it is the turning of the whole person to God." Yet as the Scripture says, "Come now and let us reason together, though your sins are like scarlet, they shall be as white as snow…" (Isa. 1:18).

We want our appeals to be used of God to move the "whole person." The bottom line is that the gospel does not permit people the luxury of indecision. We must call for a response, letting people know that the gospel requires movement on the part of the hearers.

When people close their eyes and bow their heads at altar responses, the only thought that goes through my head is, "What is God breathing in this moment?" Whatever that theme is, it becomes the key to unlock souls. I will often feel it in my gut and I can't shake it. As I address it, clear thoughts seem to flood my heart and I follow the flow. I speak in such a way as to awaken souls. God is always faithful to give me a language of the soul, then the Holy Spirit creates a transformational moment and I seize and interpret it.

PRAYING THE PRAYER

First of all, we have to be confident that God has empowered us to lead people to Christ. The reason we can be confident is two things: (1) the indwelling of the Holy Spirit, and (2) you come under the Lordship of Jesus Christ, so you've experienced that which you are bringing people into.

Lost people need to be receptive to the person sharing Jesus as well as to the gospel.

UP ON WHAT THEY HAVE DOWN

Here are some tips for sharing:

1. Be genuine in your communication. This may not seem like a super-spiritual step, but it really is; it will put people at ease. Authenticity is one of the most compelling communication characteristics in this generation.

2. Pray for guidance. Ask God to direct and lead you, even while you are talking with the person. I have developed an ability to keep both ears open; listening to what the person is talking about, but also listening to what God may be telling me.

3. Release a spirit of compassion. Let them know that you love and care about them.

4. Don't be judgmental. This generation is typically non-judgmental. We must let the Word of God become the jurisdiction for others.

5. Ask for permission. Ask if you can pray with them. If you have their permission you are more confident in leading them into the prayer of salvation.

You share Jesus with people by starting where they are at. You can't start where you want them to be; you've got to start from where they are. You can do this by finding the following:

1. Ignorance level—How much do they know about the gospel? How much do they know about Jesus, or the cross? I know some people

who have lifted their hands and responded to an altar call at a church service, and they don't really know what they're doing.

2. Interest Level—Some people are interested and give their lives to Christ, but they still want to compromise on the side. They have no intention of living a pure and sanctified life, they just respond to an altar call.

3. Hostility Level—Are they angry? Maybe they're concerned about what Christians believe. They may even be embittered because of the way they've been burned by a church or particular Christian.

4. Conviction Level—To what extent has God impressed upon the person their need to change? This may be the most important thing.

5. Past History Level—What have they gone through in their life as it relates to authority figures, Christians, and the Church?

You may not find out all of these things when you are witnessing, but they are some tools for you. These five things will help you address the resistance a person may have to the gospel.

If it's ignorance, inform them on what they need to know. If they're interested, let them know how much God loves them and how much God is interested in them. If it's hostility, you might need to apologize on behalf of the Church or a Christian who may have hurt them.

Our sensitivity to non-Christians' spiritual needs is a major factor to determining whether or not we will reach them. Lost people have to be receptive to you before they're receptive to Christ.

THE FIVE STAGES TO LEADING SOMEONE TO CHRIST

1. The "warm up" stage—This is where you engage them in conversation.

    A.   Determine their degree of openness.

    B.   Be prayerful; look to be led by the Holy Spirit.

    C.   Ask questions.

2. The "Word up" stage—Present the plan of salvation.

    A.   "Romans Road"—Scriptures from Romans that lead people to Christ:

        Romans 3:12—their condition of sin

        Romans 6:23—their consequences due to sin

        Romans 5:8—their means of reconciliation

Romans 10:9-13—their course of alteration.

B. Personal testimony or salvation/restoration testimony. For those of you who may have been born and raised in the Church, you may want to use a restoration testimony. Share about a time when God personally introduced Himself to you for the first time, or intervened in a painful situation.

C. The message of the cross—Share how Christ suffered for them personally.

D. Speak to their itch—Speak to a felt need, or something that they may share with you that is causing pain in their lives. We can tailor-make the answer to the question that they may have. Author Rick Richardson says, "Bank on the fact that people have a soul and spiritual interest and hunger."

E. Refer to the message they just heard—If you are at the altar with someone after a service, refer to the message they just heard from the pastor or speaker.

3. The "Step Up" Stage—This is the stage where you ask them to receive Christ.

A. Let the Holy Spirit draw the person to Christ according to His schedule. I used to try to hurry and get the person to make a decision and realized it was like trying to hurry a pregnant woman to have a baby. If you force it out early, it's premature and it may not live.

B. Ask them, "Is there any good reason why you should not receive Christ right now?" This is about getting them to address some issues.

C. Satan will most likely attack at this point, this is the place when someone's cell phone will go off, they'll feel some resistance, or it will all of a sudden get awkward. Satan does crazy things at the last minute. Understand that this will happen and keep your cool.

4. The "Fess Up" Stage—This is where you lead them into a confession and simple prayer out loud. It is so important that you get them to verbalize the prayer; what you're looking for is an expression of repentance and faith.

Why is it important to get them to say it out loud? Romans 10:9 says, "If you confess with your mouth the Lord Jesus and believe in your heart that God has raised Him from the dead, you will be saved." The mouth is the launching pad of the Spirit. All of the weapons of our warfare are launched through our verbal prayers.

Practically speaking, praying aloud reinforces the vividness of the memory of the person's experience. You want them to remember this momentous occasion. It will help them to recall a definite time of consciously placing faith in Jesus as Lord. This is when they know they moved from darkness into light.

You may be asking, "What should we have them pray?" About 99 percent of the time, I use Romans 10:9-10 as the basic prayer format. I say, "Say this with me. Jesus, thank You for calling my name, and I now call upon Your Name. I confess You as Lord of my life." This is a major part. It helps to have them start thanking God for moving towards them, drawing them, or opening their eyes, however you want to put it.

I then move from that thankfulness to confessing that Jesus is Lord of their lives. I say something like, "I ask You to take the steering wheel of my life, or come into my heart. I ask You to be president of my life." Have them say anything that states that Jesus is Lord.

From there I have them repent. I tell people that repenting means that you can start over. I say, "I repent of my sins." Explain to them, "If you have junky old furniture in your house, and you just bought the best new, expensive, designer furniture, what would you do? You would get out all of that old, junky furniture and make room for the new furniture."

Repentance is saying that there is a lot of old stuff that you need to get out of your life to make room for the awesome stuff that God is moving in. Repentance says, "I'm making room for the blessing."

So I say, "I repent of my sins. I'm sorry for hurting You, hurting others, and hurting myself." Again, I'm not trying to give you a formula, just ideas.

I want people to be reassured about what just happened, so I say something like, "Lord, thank You for forgiving me." You need to say that, because some people feel like they've done something so bad that Jesus could never forgive them. So I say, "I thank You for forgiving me, I thank You for loving me, and I thank You that I am now a child of

God." So by thanking God in all three areas, it hits three areas of assurance; they are now forgiven, loved, and in the family of God.

Finally, I have them close with a statement of their new commitment with God from this point on. Something like, "And I'm going to walk with You all the days of my life." Or, "I'm going to walk with You no matter what," or "Lord, I thank You that You died on the cross for me; I'm going to live for You now." Something to that effect, and then I close with, "Amen."

5. The "Follow-Up" Stage

    A.   Encourage them on what just happened. The Bible says that there is a transfer from the kingdom of darkness to the kingdom of light. Get excited for them! Tell them that they just moved from the lowest part of the universe to the highest part of the universe all in one prayer.

    B.   Pray for their needs.

    C.   Give them some growth instructions.

    D.   Pray for them—daily.

    E.   Regularly contact them for encouragement and assistance.

    F.   Connect them with a local body.

MY PRAYER FOR YOU, PROPHETIC EVANGELIST

"Lord, I ask You to place a fresh anointing upon this reader to harvest souls en mass. Let a prophetic flow open their mouth, while an evangelistic flow opens their heart. God, lead them with Heaven-sent burdens that tenderize their heart towards the lost. May boldness and brokenness characterize their walk, while You release signs and wonders in their midst.

"I pray for a hedge of protection to be raised up around them and a wall of fire to encompass them. Give them grace and miracles to confirm the word shared. Break off of them hindrances, while giving them keys to unlock the hearts of their generation. I ask for favor to go before them and loving conviction to follow them. Let friends, relatives, associates, and neighbors get saved and come to Christ consistently and allow their conversions to be lasting and impacting.

"Release divine blueprints and strategies to take campuses, workplaces, and communities, yes, even nations, for Your glory. Increase the

divine activity over the dark 'hot spots' in hearts and cities. Lord, vindicate Your name in our day and let the Lamb be glorified by the grateful praises of freshly delivered lives. Drop upon us a double-portion 'Elijah' anointing to demonstrate Your sovereignty.

    "Finally, I ask for a new breed of prophetic evangelists to be raised up, to reap in this hour. Thank You, Jesus, for blessing my friend."

Grace and Peace,
Sean Smith

MINISTRY CONTACT INFORMATION

Sean Smith Ministries- Pointblank International
PO Box 2821
San Ramon, CA 94853

Phone: 925.831.2880
Fax: 925.829.3484

http://www.seansmithministries.org